MOHSIN HAMID

CORNELSEN
SENIOR
ENGLISH
LIBRARY

The Reluctant Fundamentalist

W0041678

Cornelsen

Mohsin Hamid **The Reluctant Fundamentalist**

Herausgegeben von:
Michael Thürwächter

Verlagsredaktion:
Neil Porter

Layout und technische Umsetzung:
Annika Preyhs für Buchgestaltung+, Berlin

Umschlaggestaltung:
Cornelsen Verlag Design; Bildrecherche: Josephine Wolff

Umschlagfotos:
Lahore Fort: © Arif Ali/AFP/Getty Images
Manhattan Skyline: © Alan Songquan Deng/Shutterstock Images

Autorenfoto:
© 2007 Marco Secchi/Getty Images

Copyright © Mohsin Hamid, 2007

www.cornelsen.de

1. Auflage, 3. Druck 2014

Alle Drucke dieser Auflage sind inhaltlich unverändert
und können im Unterricht nebeneinander verwendet werden.

© 2012 Cornelsen Verlag, Berlin
© 2014 Cornelsen Schulverlage GmbH, Berlin

Das Werk und seine Teile sind urheberrechtlich geschützt.
Jede Nutzung in anderen als den gesetzlich zugelassenen Fällen bedarf der vorherigen
schriftlichen Einwilligung des Verlages.
Hinweis zu §§ 46, 52 a UrhG: Weder das Werk noch seine Teile dürfen ohne eine
solche Einwilligung eingescannt und in ein Netzwerk eingestellt oder sonst öffentlich
zugänglich gemacht werden.
Dies gilt auch für Intranets von Schulen und sonstigen Bildungseinrichtungen.

Druck: Offizin Andersen Nexö Leipzig

ISBN 978-3-06-033142-0

 Inhalt gedruckt auf säurefreiem Papier aus nachhaltiger Forstwirtschaft.

Contents

The Reluctant Fundamentalist 5

Additional Texts 137

The Author.. ..176

Abbreviations and Annotations

adj	adjective	**jdm./jdn.**	jemandem/en
adv	adverb	**n**	noun
AE	American English	**p., pp**	page, pages
ca.	circa; about	**jdm./jdn.**	jemandem/en
cf.	confer; see	**pl**	plural
derog	derogatory	**sb.**	somebody
e.g.	exempli gratia; for example	**sl**	slang
esp.	especially	**sth.**	something
fml	formal	**usu.**	usually
i.e.	id est; in other words	**v**	verb
infml	informal		

The annotations are arranged chronologically; the first time a word is used is where you will find it explained. Differences between the American spelling as used in the novel and British spelling are not given. All pronunciations given are American.

1

Excuse me, sir, but may I be of assistance? Ah, I see I have alarmed you. Do not be frightened by my beard: I am a lover of America. I noticed that you were looking for something; more than looking, in fact you seemed to be on a *mission,* and since I am both a native of
5   this city and a speaker of your language, I thought I might offer you my services.

   How did I know you were American? No, not by the color of your skin; we have a range of complexions in this country, and yours occurs often among the people of our northwest frontier. Nor was it
10   your dress that gave you away; a European tourist could as easily have purchased in Des Moines your suit, with its single vent, and your button-down shirt. True, your hair, short-cropped, and your expansive chest – the chest, I would say, of a man who bench-presses regularly, and maxes out well above two-twenty-five – are typical of
15   a certain *type* of American; but then again, sportsmen and soldiers of all nationalities tend to look alike. Instead, it was your *bearing* that allowed me to identify you, and I do not mean that as an insult, for I see your face has hardened, but merely as an observation.

   Come, tell me, what were you looking for? Surely, at this time of
20   day, only one thing could have brought you to the district of Old Anarkali – named, as you may be aware, after a courtesan immured for loving a prince – and that is the quest for the perfect cup of tea. Have I guessed correctly? Then allow me, sir, to suggest my favorite

---

8 **complexion**: natural colour of the skin on a person's face   11 **Des Moines**
[də ˈmɔɪn]: capital of the state of Iowa, USA   **vent**: *(bei Jacken und Mänteln) Schlitz
auf der Rückseite*   12 **button-down shirt**: a shirt with the ends of the collar fastened
to the shirt with buttons   13 **bench-press**: lift weights by pushing them up in front
of your chest while lying on a bench   14 **max out** (AE infml): reach the limit at
which nothing more is possible   **two-twenty-five** (AE): 102 kg (1 pound = 0.45 kg)
16 **bearing** (n): the way in which you stand, walk or behave   21 **courtesan**
[ˌkɔːrtəzən] (old use): a prostitute, esp. one with rich customers   **immure sb.**: have
sb. buried alive between walls   22 **quest** (fml): search

among these many establishments. Yes, this is the one. Its metal chairs are no better upholstered, its wooden tables are equally rough, and it is, like the others, open to the sky. But the quality of its tea, I assure you, is unparalleled.

You prefer that seat, with your back so close to the wall? Very 5 well, although you will benefit less from the intermittent breeze, which, when it does blow, makes these warm afternoons more pleasant. And will you not remove your jacket? So formal! Now *that* is not typical of Americans, at least not in my experience. And my experience is substantial: I spent four and a half years in your 10 country. Where? I worked in New York, and before that attended college in New Jersey. Yes, you are right: it *was* Princeton! Quite a guess, I must say.

What did I think of Princeton? Well, the answer to that question requires a story. When I first arrived, I looked around me at the 15 Gothic buildings – younger, I later learned, than many of the mosques of this city, but made through acid treatment and ingenious stonemasonry to look older – and thought, *This is a dream come true.* Princeton inspired in me the feeling that my life was a film in which I was the star and everything was possible. *I have access to this* 20 *beautiful campus,* I thought, *to professors who are titans in their fields and fellow students who are philosopher-kings in the making.*

I was, I must admit, overly generous in my initial assumptions about the standard of the student body. They were almost all intelligent, and many were brilliant, but whereas I was one of only 25 two Pakistanis in my entering class – two from a population of over a hundred million souls, mind you – the Americans faced much less daunting odds in the selection process. A thousand of your

---

2 **upholstered**: *gepolstert*   4 **unparalleled**: unequalled   6 **intermittent**: *sporadic*
10 **substantial**: large in amount, value or importance   16 **Gothic**: (here) neo-
Gothic, a style of architecture popular in the 19th century   17 **acid treatment**:
Säurebehandlung   **ingenious** [ɪnˈdʒiːniəs]: very clever   18 **stonemasonry**: the art of
building houses with stones   22 **be in the making**: in the process of becoming sth.
or of being made   23 **overly**: excessively   26 **entering class**: (in the USA) the first
year of university   27 **mind you**: used for emphasis   27–28 **face daunting odds**:
encounter great difficulties

compatriots were enrolled, five hundred times as many, even though your country's population was only twice that of mine. As a result, the non-Americans among us tended on average to do better than the Americans, and in my case I reached my senior year without
5 having received a single B.

Looking back now, I see the power of that system, pragmatic and effective, like so much else in America. We international students were sourced from around the globe, sifted not only by well-honed standardized tests but by painstakingly customized evaluations –
10 interviews, essays, recommendations – until the best and the brightest of us had been identified. I myself had among the top exam results in Pakistan and was besides a soccer player good enough to compete on the varsity team, which I did until I damaged my knee in my sophomore year. Students like me were given visas and
15 scholarships, complete financial aid, mind you, and invited into the ranks of the meritocracy. In return, we were expected to contribute our talents to your society, the society we were joining. And for the most part, we were happy to do so. I certainly was, at least at first.

Every fall, Princeton raised her skirt for the corporate recruiters
20 who came onto campus and – as you say in America – showed them some skin. The skin Princeton showed was good skin, of course – young, eloquent, and clever as can be – but even among all that skin, I knew in my senior year that I was something special. I was a perfect breast, if you will – tan, succulent, seemingly defiant of
25 gravity – and I was confident of getting any job I wanted.

Except one: Underwood Samson & Company. You have not heard of them? They were a valuation firm. They told their clients

1 **compatriot**: fellow countryman   **be enrolled**: officially registered as a student
5 **B**: good (according to the Anglo-Saxon grading system, in which A means
excellent and F means fail)   8 **source sb./sth.**: get sb./sth. (from a particular
place)   **sift sb.**: (here) carefully choose sb. from a group of people   **well-honed**
(adj): perfected over time   9 **customized**: made to suit the needs of the owner
12 **besides**: also, moreover   13 **varsity team**: main team of a college in a particular
sport   14 **sophomore**: second year of college   16 **meritocracy**: a system in which
the talented are chosen and moved ahead on the basis of their achievements
19 **corporate recruiter**: person from a large company looking for new employees
24 **succulent**: juicy and delicious   27 **valuation firm**: a company that makes a
professional judgement about how much money a business is worth

how much businesses were worth, and they did so, it was said, with a precision that was uncanny. They were small – a boutique, really, employing a bare minimum of people – and they paid well, offering the fresh graduate a base salary of over eighty thousand dollars. But more importantly, they gave one a robust set of skills and an exalted 5 brand name, so exalted, in fact, that after two or three years there as an analyst, one was virtually guaranteed admission to Harvard Business School. Because of this, over a hundred members of the Princeton Class of 2001 sent their grades and résumés to Underwood Samson. Eight were selected – not for jobs, I should make clear, but 10 for interviews – and one of them was me.

You seem worried. Do not be; this burly fellow is merely our waiter, and there is no need to reach under your jacket, I assume to grasp your wallet, as we will pay him later, when we are done. Would you prefer regular tea, with milk and sugar, or green tea, or perhaps 15 their more fragrant specialty, Kashmiri tea? Excellent choice. I will have the same, and perhaps a plate of jalebis as well. There. He has gone. I must admit, he is a rather intimidating chap. But irreproachably polite: you would have been surprised by the sweetness of his speech, if only you understood Urdu. 20

Where were we? Ah yes, Underwood Samson. On the day of my interview, I was uncharacteristically nervous. They had sent a single interviewer, and he received us in a room at the Nassau Inn, an ordinary room, mind you, not a suite; they knew we were sufficiently impressed already. When my turn came, I entered and found a man 25 physically not unlike yourself; he, too, had the look of a seasoned army officer. "Changez?" he said, and I nodded, for that is indeed my name. "Come on in and take a seat."

2 **uncanny**: strange and difficult to explain   4 **fresh graduate**: person who has just left university   5 **exalted**: of high level   12 **burly**: big, strong and heavy 16 **fragrant** ['freɪgrənt]: having a pleasant smell   17 **jalebi**: type of sweet popular in south Asia   18 **intimidating**: frightening in a way that makes other people less confident   19 **irreproachable**: free from fault and impossible to criticize 20 **Urdu**: one of Pakistan's national languages, which is also spoken by many Muslims in India   23 **Nassau Inn**: exclusive hotel in Princeton   26 **seasoned**: having a lot of experience of a particular activity

His name was Jim, he told me, and I had precisely fifty minutes to convince him to offer me a job. "Sell yourself," he said. "What makes you special?" I began with my transcript, pointing out that I was on track to graduate *summa cum laude,* that I had, as I have mentioned,
5　yet to receive a single B. "I'm sure you're smart," he said, "but none of the people I'm talking to today has any Bs." This, for me, was an unsettling revelation. I told him that I was tenacious, that after injuring my knee I had made it through physiotherapy in half the time the doctors expected, and while I could no longer play varsity
10　soccer, I could once again run a mile in less than six minutes. "That's good," he said, and for the first time it seemed to me I had made something of an impression on him, when he added, "but what else?"

I fell silent. I am, as you can see, normally quite happy to chat,
15　but in that moment I did not know what to say. I watched him watch me, trying to understand what he was looking for. He glanced down at my résumé, which was lying between us on the table, and then back up again. His eyes were cold, a pale blue, and *judgmental,* not in the way that word is normally used, but in the sense of being
20　professionally appraising, like a jeweler's when he inspects out of curiosity a diamond he intends neither to buy nor to sell. Finally, after some time had passed – it could not have been more than a minute, but it felt longer – he said, "Tell me something. Where are you from?"
25　I said I was from Lahore, the second largest city of Pakistan, ancient capital of the Punjab, home to nearly as many people as New York, layered like a sedimentary plain with the accreted history of

---

3 **transcript** (AE): official record of a student's work that shows the courses they have taken and the marks they have achieved   3–4 **be on track**: be doing the right thing in order to achieve a particular result   4 **summa cum laude** [ˌsʌmə kʌm ˈlɔːdi] (Latin): the highest level of achievement that students can reach when they finish their studies at university   7 **tenacious**: a person that doesn't give up easily 18 **judgmental**: judging people and criticizing them too quickly   20 **appraise sb.**: make a formal judgment about the value of sb.'s work   26 **the Punjab**: a historical region now divided between India and Pakistan   27 **sedimentary plain**: a large area of flat fertile land   **accreted** (adj): slowly getting bigger over time

invaders from the Aryans to the Mongols to the British. He merely nodded. Then he said, "And are you on financial aid?"

I did not answer him at once. I knew there were subjects interviewers were not permitted to broach – religion, for example, and sexual orientation – and I suspected financial aid was one of these. But that was not why I hesitated; I hesitated because his question made me feel uncomfortable. Then I said, "Yes." "And isn't it harder," he asked, "for international students to get in if they apply for aid?" Again I said, "Yes." "So," he said, "you must have really needed the money." And for the third time, I said, "Yes."

Jim leaned back in his chair and crossed his legs at the knee, just as you are doing now. Then he said, "You're polished, well-dressed. You have this sophisticated accent. Most people probably assume you're rich where you come from." It was not a question, so I made no reply. "Do your friends here know," he went on, "that your family couldn't afford to send you to Princeton without a scholarship?"

This was, as I have said, the most important of my interviews, and I knew moreover that I ought to remain calm, but I was getting annoyed, and I had had enough of this line of questioning. So I said, "Excuse me, Jim, but is there a point to all this?" It came out more aggressively than I intended, my voice rising and taking on an edge. "So they don't know," Jim said. He smiled and went on, "You have a temper. I like that. I went to Princeton, too. Class of '81. *Summa cum laude.*" He winked. "I was the first guy from my family to go to college. I worked a night shift in Trenton to pay my way, far enough from campus that people wouldn't find out. So I get where you're coming from, Changez. You're hungry, and that's a good thing in my book."

1 **Aryans**: the ancient peoples who moved from Central Asia into India   **Mongols**: Eastern Asian people who conquered much of Central Asia   4 **broach sth.**: begin talking about sth. that is difficult to discuss, because it is embarrassing, etc.
12 **polished**: elegant and confident   13 **sophisticated**: cultivated and giving the appearance of knowledge   21 **edge**: a sharp tone of voice, usu. showing anger
22–23 **have a temper**: get angry easily   25 **Trenton**: city near Princeton
26–27 **get where sb. is coming from** (AE infml): understand sb. well
27–28 **in my book** (infml): as far as I am concerned, in my opinion

I was, I must confess, caught off balance. I did not know how to react. But I did know that I was impressed with Jim; he had, after all, seen through me in a few minutes more clearly than had many people who had known me for years. I could understand why he would be effective at valuations, and why – by extension – his firm had come to be highly regarded in this field. I was also pleased that he had found in me something he prized, and my confidence, until now shaken by our encounter, began to recover.

It is worth, if you will permit me, my indulging in a minor digression at this point. I am not poor; far from it: my great-grandfather, for example, was a barrister with the means to endow a school for the Muslims of the Punjab. Like him, my grandfather and father both attended university in England. Our family home sits on an acre of land in the middle of Gulberg, one of the most expensive districts of this city. We employ several servants, including a driver and a gardener – which would, in America, imply that we were a family of great wealth.

But we are not rich. The men and women – yes, the women, too – of my household are working people, professionals. And the half-century since my great-grandfather's death has not been a prosperous one for professionals in Pakistan. Salaries have not risen in line with inflation, the rupee has declined steadily against the dollar, and those of us who once had substantial family estates have seen them divided and subdivided by each – larger – subsequent generation. So my grandfather could not afford what his father could, and my father could not afford what *his* father could, and when the time came to send me to college, the money simply was not there.

---

1 **be caught off balance**: make sb. surprised and thus worried   5 **by extension** (fml): taking the argument or situation one stage further   9 **indulge in sth.**: allow yourself to do sth. that you like   10 **digression**: talking about sth. that is not the main point of what you are trying to say   11 **barrister** (BE): a lawyer who can represent people in a court of law   **means** (pl): the money a person has   **endow sth.**: give a large sum of money to sth. (e.g. a school or another institution)   14 **acre** ['eɪkə]: ca. 4050 square metres   **Gulberg**: a residential and commercial area of Lahore   16 **imply sth.**: suggest that sth. is true   19 **professional** (n): person with a job that requires a high degree of training and education   21 **prosperous**: rich and well-off

But status, as in any traditional, class-conscious society, declines more slowly than wealth. So we retain our Punjab Club membership. We continue to be invited to the functions and weddings and parties of the city's elite. And we look with a mixture of disdain and envy upon the rising class of entrepreneurs – owners of businesses legal 5 and illegal – who power through the streets in their BMW SUVs. Our situation is, perhaps, not so different from that of the old European aristocracy in the nineteenth century, confronted by the ascendance of the bourgeoisie. Except, of course, that we are part of a broader malaise afflicting not only the formerly rich but much of 10 the formerly middle-class as well: a growing inability to purchase what we previously could.

Confronted with this reality, one has two choices: pretend all is well or work hard to restore things to what they were. I chose both. At Princeton, I conducted myself in public like a young prince, 15 generous and carefree. But I also, as quietly as I could, held down three on-campus jobs – in infrequently visited locations, such as the library of the Program in Near Eastern Studies – and prepared for my classes throughout the night. Most people I met were taken in by my public persona. Jim was not. But fortunately, where I saw shame, 20 he saw opportunity. And he was, in some ways but not in all – as I would later come to understand – correct.

Ah, our tea has arrived! Do not look so suspicious. I assure you, sir, nothing untoward will happen to you, not even a runny stomach. After all, it is not as if it has been *poisoned*. Come, if it makes you 25 more comfortable, let me switch my cup with yours. Just so. How much sugar would you like? None? Very unusual, but I will not insist. Do try these sticky, orange sweets – jalebis – but be careful,

---

1 **class-conscious**: having a strict division between social classes   4 **disdain**: the feeling that sb./sth. is not good enough to deserve your respect or attention
6 **SUV = sport utility vehicle**: a large vehicle which is designed for rough ground but which is often used in cities   9 **ascendance**: rise   **bourgeoisie**: the middle classes in society   10 **malaise**: sickness, problem   **afflict sb./sth.**: affect sb./sth. in an unpleasant or harmful way   15 **conduct yourself** (fml): behave in a particular way   16 **hold sth. down**: keep sth. (esp. a job) for some time   20 **persona**: the image or personality that a person presents to other people   24 **untoward**: unexpected and usually unpleasant   24 **runny stomach** (infml): *Durchfall*

they are hot! I see you approve. Yes, they are delicious. It is curious how a cup of tea can be refreshing even on a warm day such as this – a mystery, really – but there you have it.

I was telling you about my interview with Underwood Samson,
5 and how Jim had found me to be, as he put it, *hungry*. I waited to see what he would say next, and what he said next was this: "All right, Changez, let's test you out. I'm going to give you a business case, a company I want you to value. You can ask me anything you need to know – think Twenty Questions – and you can do your calculations
10 with that pencil and paper. Ready?" I said that I was, and he continued: "I'm going to throw you a curve ball. You're going to need to get creative here. The company is simple. It has only one service line: instantaneous travel. You step into its terminal in New York, and you immediately reappear in its terminal in London. Like
15 a transporter on *Star Trek*. Get it? Good. Let's go."

I would like to think that I was, in that moment, outwardly calm, but inside I was panicking. How does one value a fictitious, fantastic company such as the one he had just described? Where does one even begin? I had no idea. I looked at Jim, but he did not seem to be
20 joking. So I inhaled and shut my eyes. There was a mental state I used to attain when I was playing soccer: my self would disappear, and I would be free, free of doubts and limits, free to focus on nothing but the game. When I entered this state I felt unstoppable. Sufi mystics and Zen masters would, I suspect, understand the
25 feeling. Possibly, ancient warriors did something similar before they went into battle, ritualistically accepting their impending death so they could function unencumbered by fear.

I entered this state in the interview. My essence was focused on finding my way through the case. I started by asking questions to

---

1 **hot**: *schaf*   11 **curve ball**: (in baseball) a ball thrown with a spin so it curves in the air; (here) a difficult and unexpected problem to resolve   13 **instantaneous**: happening immediately   15 **Star Trek**: TV series   24 **Sufi** (n): a member of a Muslim group which tries to seek a deep personal bond with God   **mystic**: a person who tries to become united with God through prayer and meditation   **Zen**: school of Buddhist thought which seeks self-enlightenment   26 **impending**: that will happen soon   27 **unencumbered**: untroubled, not slowed down   28 **essence**: (here) a person's whole being

understand the technology: how scalable it was, how reliable, how safe. Then I asked Jim about the environment: if there were any direct competitors, what the regulators might do, if any suppliers were particularly critical. Then I went into the cost side to figure out what expenses we would have to cover. And last I looked at revenues,   5 using the Concorde for comparison, as an example of the price premium and demand one gets for cutting travel time in half, and then estimating how much more one would get for cutting it to zero. Once I had done all that, I projected profits out into the future and discounted them to net present value. And in the end, I arrived at a   10 number.

"Two point three billion dollars," I said. Jim was silent for a while. Then he shook his head. "Wildly overoptimistic," he said. "Your assumptions on customers adopting this thing are way too high. Would you be willing to step into a machine, be dematerialized, and   15 then recomposed thousands of miles away? This is exactly the kind of hyped-up bullshit our clients pay Underwood Samson to see through." I hung my head. "But," Jim continued, "your approach was right on. You have what it takes. All you need is training and experience." He extended his hand. "You've got an offer. We'll give   20 you one week to decide."

At first I did not believe him. I asked if he was serious, if there was not a second round for me to pass. "We're a small firm," he said. "We don't waste time. Besides, I'm in charge of analyst recruiting. I don't need another opinion." I noticed his hand was still hanging in   25 the air between us, and – fearful it might be withdrawn – I reached out and shook it. His grip was firm and seemed to communicate to

1 **scalable**: able to expand to deal with increased use   3 **regulator**: a person or an organization that officially controls an area of business or industry and makes sure that it is operating fairly   5 **revenue**: the money that a company, etc. receives from its business   6 **Concorde**: supersonic jet that was in service from 1976 to 2003 6–7 **price premium**: the price people are willing to pay for a superior brand 7 **demand** (n): the desire or need of customers for goods   10 **discount sth.**: remove sth. (esp. an amount of money) from the original price   **net** (adj): what remains after all deductions have been made, e.g. taxes, expenses   17 **hyped-up** (infml): getting more attention than it deserves due to advertising, etc.   24 **be in charge of sth.**: have responsibility for sth.

me, in that moment, that Underwood Samson had the potential to transform my life as surely as it had transformed his, making my concerns about money and status things of the distant past.

I walked back to my dormitory – Edwards Hall, it was called –
5 later that same afternoon. The sky was a brilliant blue, so different from the orange, dusty sky above us today, and I felt something well up inside me, a sense of pride so strong that it made me lift my head and yell, as much to my own surprise as I am sure it was to the other students passing by: "Thank you, God!"

10 Yes, it was exhilarating. *That*, in an admittedly longwinded fashion, is how I think, looking back, about Princeton. Princeton made everything possible for me. But it did not, *could* not, make me forget such things as how much I enjoy the tea in this, the city of my birth, steeped long enough to acquire a rich, dark color, and made
15 creamy with fresh, full-fat milk. It is excellent, no? I see you have finished yours. Allow me to pour you another cup.

---

4 **dormitory**: (in a school, etc.) house in which students live   6–7 **well up**: (of an emotion) rise to the surface   10 **long-winded**: continuing for too long   14 **steep sth. in sth.**: (here) leave sth. (e.g. the tea) for some time in sth. (e.g. the hot water)

2

Do you see those girls, walking there, in jeans speckled with paint? Yes, they *are* attractive. And how different they look from the women of that family sitting at the table beside ours, in their traditional dress. The National College of Arts is not far – it is, as a matter of fact, only around the corner – and its students often come here for a 5 cup of tea, just as we are doing now. I see one in particular has caught your eye; she is indeed a beauty. Tell me, sir, have you left behind a love – male or female, I do not presume to know your preference, although the intensity of your gaze suggests the latter – in your homeland? 10

Your shrug is inscrutable, but I will be more forthcoming. I did leave behind a love, and her name was Erica. We met the summer after we graduated, part of a group of Princetonians who had decided to holiday together in Greece. She and the others were members of the university's most prestigious eating club, Ivy, and were traveling 15 courtesy of gifts from their parents or dividends from their trust funds, which they were now of an age to access; I had cooked my own meals in the basement kitchen of my dormitory and was there thanks to my sign-on bonus from Underwood Samson. I was friendly with one of the Ivy men, Chuck, from my days on the soccer team, 20 and was well-liked as an exotic acquaintance by some of the others, whom I had met through him.

1 **speckled**: with little spots   8 **presume**: (here) say sth. about which you have no knowledge   11 **shrug** (n): *Achselzucken*   **inscrutable**: not showing any emotion, so a person's thoughts and feelings are hard to know   **forthcoming** (adj): willing to give information about sth.   15 **prestigious**: respected and admired   **eating club**: university social club for rich students   16 **courtesy of**: paid for, provided by **dividend**: the sum from its profits that a company pays to its share owners 16–17 **trust fund**: money that is controlled for sb. by an organization or a group of people   19 **sign-on bonus**: money that is given to a person when he or she signs a work contract

We assembled in Athens, having arrived on different flights, and when I first saw Erica, I could not prevent myself from offering to carry her backpack – so stunningly *regal* was she. Her hair was piled up like a tiara on her head, and her navel – ah, what a navel: made
5 firm, I would later learn, by years of tae kwon do – was visible beneath a short T-shirt bearing an image of Chairman Mao. We were introduced, she smiled as she shook my hand – whether because she found me irresistibly refined or oddly anachronistic, I did not know – and then we headed off with the group to the port city of Piraeus.

10 It was immediately apparent that I would not have, in my wooing of Erica, the field to myself. In fact, no sooner had we set sail on our ferry to the islands than did a young man – a tooth dangling on a string of leather in front of his bare, but meagerly muscled, chest – begin to strum his guitar and serenade her from across the deck.
15 "What language is that?" she asked me, leaning close enough for her breath to tickle my ear. "English, I believe," I replied after much concentration. "As a matter of fact, it is Bryan Adams, 'Summer of '69.'" She laughed. "You're right," she said, politely lowering her voice to add, "Wow, he's terrible!" I was inclined to agree, but now
20 that I knew the troubadour posed no threat, I chose to maintain a magnanimous silence instead.

A more serious challenge would come from Chuck's good – and similarly monosyllabically monikered – friend Mike, who, the next day, as we sat in a restaurant overhanging the lip of the shattered
25 volcano that is the island of Santorini, casually extended his arm along the back of Erica's chair and remained in that position, which surely became uncomfortable, for the better part of an hour. Erica made no sign that she wished him to remove his arm, but I drew

---

1 **assemble**: (here) meet, get together   3 **regal** ['riːɡəl]: impressive, like of a king or a queen   4 **tiara** [tiˈærə]: a piece of jewellery worn on the head like a crown
navel: *Bauchnabel*   6 **Mao Zedong** (1893–1976): leader of the Chinese revolution and Chairman of the Communist Party of China (1943–1976)   8 **refined** (adj): polite, well educated   **anachronistic**: old-fashioned   10 **woo**: try to persuade a woman to go out with you   12 **dangle**: hang loosely   13 **meager**: thin
14 **serenade sb.** (v): sing or play music to sb. you love   19 **inclined to do sth.**: wanting to do sth.   21 **magnanimous** [mæɡˈnænɪməs]: kind, generous and forgiving   23 **monikered**: named   25 **casual**: *lässig*

some consolation from the fact that throughout the dinner she listened *intently* when I spoke, smiling from time to time and training her green eyes upon me. Afterwards, however, on the walk to our pension, she and Mike trailed behind the rest of us, and that night I found it difficult to sleep. 5

In the morning, I was relieved to see that she came down to breakfast *before* Mike – not with him – and I was also pleased that we appeared to be the first two of our group to be awake. She spread jam on a croissant, gave half to me, and said, "You know what I'd like to do?" I asked her what. "I'd like to stay here by myself," she 10 said, "rent a room on one of these islands and just write." I told her she should, but she shook her head. "I wouldn't last a week," she said. "I'm not good at being alone. But you, on the other hand," and here she tilted her head and crossed her arms, "I think you'd be fine." 15

I have never, to the best of my knowledge, had any fear of solitude, and so I shrugged in assent and said, by way of explanation, "When I was a child, there were eight of us, eight cousins, all in the same compound – a single boundary wall surrounded the plot of land my grandfather left to his sons, you see – and we had between 20 us as many as three dogs and, for a time, a duck." She laughed, and then she said, "So being alone was a luxury, huh?" I nodded. "You give off this strong sense of home," she said. "You know that? This I'm-from-a-big-family vibe. It's nice. It makes you feel solid." I was pleased – even though I was not sure I fully understood – and said 25 thank you for want of anything better to say. Then, hesitantly because I did not wish to be too forward, I asked, "And you, do you feel solid?"

She considered this and said, with what I thought was a trace of sadness in her voice, "Sometimes, but no, not really." Before I could 30 respond we were joined by Chuck, and then by Mike, and the

---

1 **consolation**: *Trost*   2 **intently** (adv): giving all your attention to sth.   2–3 **train sb's eyes on you**: (here) make sb. look at you   4 **trail behind**: be slower than the others   14 **tilt sth.**: *etwas schräg legen*   17 **solitude**: being alone   **assent** (n): agreement   19 **compound** (n): an area surrounded by a fence or wall   24 **solid**: stable, reliable   26 **for want of sth.**: because of a lack of sth.   29 **trace** (n): a very small amount of sth.

conversation turned to beaches and hangovers and the timings of ferries. But when I looked at Erica and she looked back at me, I felt we both understood that something had been exchanged between us, the first invitation to a friendship, perhaps, and so I waited
5 patiently for an opportunity to resume our discussion.

Such an opportunity would not come for quite some time – not until several days later, as a matter of fact. You might imagine I grew frustrated with the wait, but you must remember: I had never in my life had a vacation like this one. We rented motor scooters and
10 purchased straw mats to spread on beaches of black volcanic sand, which the sun had made too hot for bare skin; we stayed in the rooms of quaint houses let out in the summertime by elderly couples to tourists; we ate grilled octopus and drank sparkling water and red wine. I had not before this been to Europe or even swum in the sea –
15 Lahore is, as you know, a ninety-minute journey by air from the coast – and so I gave in to the pleasures of being among this wealthy young fellowship.

I will admit that there were *details* which annoyed me. The ease with which they parted with money, for example, thinking nothing
20 of the occasional – but not altogether infrequent – meal costing perhaps fifty dollars a head. Or their self-righteousness in dealing with those whom they had paid for a service. "But you *told* us," they would say to Greeks twice their age, before insisting things be done their way. I, with my finite and depleting reserve of cash and my
25 traditional sense of deference to one's seniors, found myself wondering by what quirk of human history my companions – many of whom I would have regarded as upstarts in my own country, so devoid of refinement were they – were in a position to conduct themselves in the world as though they were its ruling class.

---

10 **purchase sth.**: buy sth.   12 **quaint**: picturesque, attractive in an unusual or old-fashioned way   **let out sth.**: rent out sth. (esp. a flat or house) for a short period of time   21 **self-righteousness**: the behaviour as if what you say or do is always morally right   24 **finite**: having a definite limit or fixed amount
depleting (adj): shrinking, becoming smaller   25 **deference**: *Respekt, Ehrerbietigkeit*
26 **quirk**: *Laune*   27 **upstart**: *Empörkömmling*   28 **be devoid of sth.**: lack sth. completely   28–29 **conduct yourself**: behave

But it may be that I am inclined to exaggerate these irritants in retrospect, knowing the course my relationship with your country would later take. Besides, the rest of the group was for me mere background; in the foreground shimmered Erica, and observing her gave me enormous satisfaction. She had told me that she hated to be ⁵ alone, and I came to notice that she rarely was. She attracted people to her; she had presence, an uncommon *magnetism*. Documenting her effect on her habitat, a naturalist would likely have compared her to a lioness: strong, sleek, and invariably surrounded by her pride. ¹⁰

Yet one got the sense that she existed internally at a degree of remove from those around her. Not that she was aloof; she was, in fact, friendly in disposition. But one felt that some part of her – and this, perhaps, was a not insubstantial component of her appeal – was out of reach, lost in thoughts unsaid. Suffice it to say that in ¹⁵ relationship to the contemporary female icons of your country, she belonged more to the camp of Paltrow than to that of Spears.

But my cultural reference has fallen on deaf ears! You appear distracted, sir; those pretty girls from the National College of Arts have clearly recaptured your attention. Or are you watching that ²⁰ man, the one with the beard far longer than mine, who has stopped to stand beside them? You think he will scold them for the inappropriateness of their dress – their T-shirts and jeans? I suspect not: those girls seem comfortable in this area and are likely to come here often, while he looks out of place. Moreover, among the many ²⁵ rules that govern the bazaars of Lahore is this: if a woman is harassed by a man, she has the right to appeal to the brotherly instincts of the

1 **irritant**: sth. that makes you annoyed   1–2 **in retrospect**: looking back at a past event   8 **habitat**: the place where a particular type of animal or plant is normally found   **naturalist**: biologist   9 **sleek**: *geschmeidig*   **invariably**: always   10 **pride**: group of lions   11–12 **a degree of remove**: slightly distant   12 **aloof**: not friendly or interested in other people   13 **disposition**: character, temperament   14 **appeal**: attractiveness   15 **suffice it to say** [sə'faɪs]: used to suggest that although you could say more, what you do say will be enough to explain what you mean   17 **camp**: *Lager*   **Gwyneth Paltrow** (born 1972): American actress   **Britney Spears** (born 1981): American singer   22 **scold sb.**: speak angrily to sb., esp. a child, because they have done sth. wrong   26 **harass sb.**: attack or annoy sb. through actions or words   27 **appeal to sb.**: make a serious request to sb.

mob, and the mob is known to beat men who annoy their sisters. *There,* sir, you see? He has moved on. He was merely staring at something he found intriguing, much as you are, but in your case, of course, with considerably more discretion.

5   As for myself, that summer in Greece with Erica, I tried not to stare. But towards the end of our holiday, on the island of Rhodes, I could not help myself. You have not been to Rhodes? You must go. It seemed to me unlike the other islands we had visited. Its cities were fortified, protected by ancient castles; they guarded against the
10 Turks, much like the army and navy and air force of modern Greece, part of a wall against the East that still stands. How strange it was for me to think I grew up on the other side!

But that is neither here nor there. I was telling you about the moment when I was forced to stare. We were lying on the beach, and
15 many of the European women nearby were, as usual, sunbathing topless – a practice I wholeheartedly supported, but which the women among us Princetonians, unfortunately, had thus far failed to embrace – when I noticed Erica was untying the straps of her bikini. And then, as I watched, only an arm's length away, she bared her
20 breasts to the sun.

A moment later – no, you are right: I am being dishonest; it was *more* than a moment – she turned her head to the side and saw me staring at her. A number of possible alternatives presented themselves: I could suddenly avert my eyes, thereby proving not
25 only that I had been staring but that I was uncomfortable with her nudity; I could, after a brief pause, casually move my gaze away, as though the sight of her breasts had been the most natural thing in the world; I could keep staring, honestly communicating in this way my admiration for what she had revealed; or I could, through well-
30 timed literary allusion, draw her attention to the fact that there was a passage in *Mr. Palomar* that captured perfectly my dilemma.

---

1 **annoy sb.**: make sb. uncomfortable by bothering them   2 **stare at sth.**: look at sth. intensely for a long time   3 **intriguing** (adj): very interesting because of being unusual   9 **fortified** (adj): having thick, high walls to protect it from attacks
24 **avert your eyes from sth.**: turn your eyes away from sth. you don't want to see
31 **Mr. Palomar**: philosophical novel (1983) by Italo Calvino

But I did none of these things. Instead, I blushed and said, "Hello." She smiled – with uncharacteristic shyness, it seemed to me – and replied, "Hi." I nodded, tried to think of something else to say, failed, and said, "Hello," again. As soon as I had done this, I wanted to disappear; I knew I sounded unbelievably foolish. She   5 started to laugh, her small breasts bouncing, and said, "I'm going for a swim." But then, as she walked away, she half-turned and added, "You want to come?"

I followed her, watching the muscles of her lower back tense delicately to stabilize her spine. We reached the water; it was warm   10 and perfectly clear, round pebbles and the flash of little fish visible below the surface. We slipped inside, she swam out into the bay with powerful strokes, and then she treaded water until I had caught up with her. For a time we were both silent and I felt our slippery legs graze each other as we churned the sea. "I don't think," she said   15 finally, "I've ever met someone our age as polite as you." "Polite?" I said, less than radiant with joy. She smiled. "I don't mean it that way," she said. "Not *boring* polite. Respectful polite. You give people their space. I really like that. It's unusual."

We continued bobbing face to face, and I formed the impression   20 that she was waiting for me to say something in reply, but words had abandoned me. Instead, my thoughts were engaged in a struggle to maintain a facial expression that would not appear idiotic. She turned and began to swim back to shore, keeping her head above water. I pulled alongside and – claiming victory at last over my   25 cowering tongue – said, "Shall we return to town for a drink?" To which she replied, with a raised eyebrow and in an accent not normally her own, "I would be delighted to do so, sir."

On the beach she put on a shirt – a gentleman's shirt, I still remember, blue and fraying at the tips of the collar – and stuffed her   30 towel and bikini top into a bag. None of our companions wanted to

---

1 **blush**: turn suddenly red in the face, usually in an embarrassing moment
9 **tense**: *anspannen*   10 **spine**: backbone   13 t**read water**: keep floating by moving your arms and legs   17 **radiant** ['reɪdiənt]: showing great happiness
20 **bob** (v): move up and down in water   22 **abandon sb./sth.**: leave sb./sth.
26 **cower**: hide in a cowardly way   30 **fray**: start to come apart

join us, there being at least another hour of tan-inducing sunlight remaining in the day, and so we two made our way to the road and caught a bus. As we sat side by side, I could not help but notice that her bare leg was less than an inch from where I was resting my hand
5 on my thigh.

It is remarkable, I must say, how being in Pakistan heightens one's sensitivity to the sight of a woman's body. Do you not agree? That bearded man – who even now, sir, continues from time to time to attract your wary gaze – is himself unable to stop glancing over his
10 shoulder at those girls, fifty yards away from him. Yet they are exposing only the flesh of the neck, the face, and the lower three-quarters of the arm! It is the effect of scarcity; one's rules of propriety make one *thirst* for the improper. Moreover, once sensitized in this manner, one numbs only slowly, if at all; I had by the summer of my
15 trip to Greece spent four years in America already – and had experienced all the intimacies college students commonly experience – but still I remained acutely aware of visible female skin.

It was in order to prevent myself from impolitely focusing on Erica's wheat-colored limbs that I asked her if her shirt had belonged
20 to her father. "No," she said, rubbing the fabric between her thumb and forefinger, "it was my boyfriend's." "Ah," I said, "I did not know you had a boyfriend." "He died last year," she said. "His name was Chris." I said I was sorry and told her that it was a fine shirt; Chris had had excellent taste. She agreed, saying that he had been quite
25 the dandy, and rather vain even in hospital. His nurses had been charmed by him: he was a good-looking boy with what she described as an *Old World* appeal.

Arriving in town, we found a café near the harbor with tables shaded by blue-and-white umbrellas. She ordered a beer; I did the

---

1 **tan-inducing**: causing a brown skin from sunbathing   6 **heighten sth.**: make sth. stronger   7 **sensitivity**: awareness   9 **wary**: cautious, suspicious   10 **yard**: unit of measurement (ca. 0.9 m)   12 **scarcity**: lack of sth.   **propriety** [prə'praɪəti]: acceptable moral and social behaviour   13 **sensitize sb.**: make sb. more aware of sth.   14 **numb** (v): feel less intensely   16 **intimacy**: the state of having a close personal relationship with sb.   17 **acutely aware of sth.** [ə'kjuːtli]: noticing or feeling sth. very strongly   19 **wheat**: *Weizen*   25 **dandy**: a man who cares a lot about his clothes and appearance   **vain**: *eitel*

same. "So what's Pakistan like?" she asked. I told her Pakistan was many things, from seaside to desert to farmland stretched between rivers and canals; I told her that I had driven with my parents and my brother to China on the Karakoram Highway, passing along the bottoms of valleys higher than the tops of the Alps; I told her that 5 alcohol was illegal for Muslims to buy and so I had a Christian bootlegger who delivered booze to my house in a Suzuki pickup. She listened to me speak with a series of smiles, as though she were sipping at my descriptions and finding them to her taste. Then she said, "You miss home." 10

I shrugged. I often did miss home, but in that moment I was content to be where I was. She took out her notebook – it was bound with soft, orange leather; I had previously seen her scribbling in it during moments of repose – and passing it to me with a pencil said, "What does your writing look like?" I said, "Urdu is similar to Arabic, 15 but we have more letters." She said, "Show me," and so I did. "It's beautiful," she said, meeting my eyes. "What's it mean?" "This is your name," I replied, "and this, underneath, is mine."

We stayed at our table, talking as the sun set, and she told me about Chris. They had grown up together – in facing apartments, 20 children the same age with no siblings – and were best friends well before their first kiss, which happened when they were six but was not repeated until they were fifteen. He had a collection of European comic books with which they were obsessed, and they used to spend hours at home reading them and making their own: Chris drawing, 25 Erica writing. They were both admitted to Princeton, but he had not come because he was diagnosed with lung cancer – he had had *one* cigarette, she said with a smile, but only the day after he received the results of his biopsy – and she had made sure she never had classes on a Friday so she could spend three days a week in New York with 30 him. He died three years later, at the end of the spring semester of

4 **Karakoram Highway**: highest paved highway in the world that connects China and Pakistan   7 **bootlegger**: illegal distiller/seller of alcohol   **booze** (sl): alcohol
9 **sip (at) sth.**: drink sth. by taking a very small amount each time   14 **repose**
(fml): rest, relaxation   20 **facing**: that are in front of each other   29 **biopsy**
['baɪɑːpsi]: examination of tissue from the body of a sick person in order to find out what the problem is

her junior year. "So I kind of miss home, too," she said. "Except my home was a guy with long, skinny fingers."

Later that evening, when we went out for dinner with the group, Erica chose the seat opposite mine. Chuck made all of us laugh with
5 a series of uncanny impersonations – my mannerisms were, in my opinion, somewhat exaggerated, but the others were spot on – and then he went around the table and asked each of us to reveal our dream for what we would most like to be. When my turn came, I said I hoped one day to be the dictator of an Islamic republic with
10 nuclear capability; the others appeared shocked, and I was forced to explain that I had been joking. Erica alone smiled; she seemed to understand my sense of humor.

Erica said that she wanted to be a novelist. Her creative thesis had been a work of long fiction that had won an award at Princeton; she
15 intended to revise it for submission to literary agents and would see how they responded. Normally, Erica spoke little of herself, and tonight, when she did so, it was in a slightly lowered voice and with her eyes often on me. I felt – despite the presence of our companions, whose attention, as always, she managed to capture – that she was
20 sharing with me an intimacy, and this feeling grew stronger when, after observing me struggle, she helped me separate the flesh from the bones of my fish without my having to ask.

Nothing physical happened between Erica and me in Greece; we did not so much as hold hands. But she gave me her number in New
25 York, to which we were both returning, and she offered to help me settle in. For my part, I was content: I had struck up an acquaintance with a woman with whom I was well and truly smitten, and my excitement about the adventures my new life held for me had never been more pronounced.

---

5 **uncanny**: (here) surprisingly and strangely accurate   **impersonation**: the act of mimicking sb.'s voice and behaviour   **mannerism**: a particular habit or way of speaking sb. has   6 **spot on** (adj, infml): exactly right   13 **creative thesis**: project about a topic in a person's university study course but which is not academic (i.e. it can be a film, novel, etc.)   26 **strike up sth.**: start sth.   27 **smitten with/by sb.**: suddenly feeling that you are in love with sb.   29 **pronounced**: very noticeable, obvious

But what is that? Ah, your mobile phone! I have not previously seen its like; it is, I suspect, one of those models capable of communicating via satellite when no ground coverage is available. Will you not answer it? I assure you, sir, I will do my *utmost* to avoid eavesdropping on your conversation. But you are opting to write a   5 text message instead; very wise: often a few words are more than sufficient. As for myself, I am quite happy to wait as you navigate the keys. After all, those girls from the National College of Arts have only just finished their tea, and the pleasure of their presence on this street will persist for a few moments longer before they disappear –   10 as inevitably they must – from view around that corner.

4 **do your utmost**: do everything possible   5 **eavesdrop on sth.**: listen secretly to sth.   10 **persist**: continue

3

We locals treasure these last days of what passes for spring here in Lahore; the sun, although hot, has such a soothing effect. Or, I should say, it has such a soothing effect on *us*, for you, sir, continue to appear ill at ease. I hope you will not mind my saying so, but the
5   frequency and purposefulness with which you glance about – a steady tick-tick-tick seeming to beat in your head as you move your gaze from one point to the next – brings to mind the behavior of an animal that has ventured too far from its lair and is now, in unfamiliar surroundings, uncertain whether it is predator or prey!

10   Come, relinquish your foreigner's sense of being watched. Observe instead how the shadows have lengthened. Soon they will shut to traffic the gates at either end of this market, transforming Old Anarkali into a pedestrian-only piazza. In fact, they have begun. Will the police arrest those boys on their motor scooter? Only if they
15   can catch them! And already they are streaking away, making good their escape. But they will be the last to do so. The gates are now being locked, as you can see, and those gaps that remain are too narrow for anything wider than a man.

    You will have noticed that the newer districts of Lahore are poorly
20   suited to the needs of those who must walk. In their spaciousness – with their public parks and wide, tree-lined boulevards – they enforce an ancient hierarchy that comes to us from the countryside: the superiority of the mounted man over the man on foot. But here, where we sit, and in the even older districts that lie between us and
25   the River Ravi – the congested, mazelike heart of this city – Lahore is

---

1 **local** (n): *Einheimische/r* 2 **soothing**: calming, relaxing 4 **ill at ease**: feeling uncomfortable 8 **venture**: go somewhere exciting or dangerous **lair**: a wild animal's sleeping or hiding place 9 **predator**: *Raubtier* **prey**: *Beute*
10 **relinquish sth.**: give sth. up 15 **streak away**: move away quickly **make good sth.**: carry out sth. successfully 19–20 p**oorly suited to sth.**: not made for sth.
23 **mounted**: sitting on a horse 25 **congested**: full of traffic **maze**: labyrinth

more democratically *urban*. Indeed, in these places it is the man with four wheels who is forced to dismount and become part of the crowd.

Like Manhattan? Yes, precisely! And that was one of the reasons why for me moving to New York felt – so unexpectedly – like coming home. But there were other reasons as well: the fact that Urdu was spoken by taxicab drivers; the presence, only two blocks from my East Village apartment, of a samosa- and channa-serving establishment called the Pak-Punjab Deli; the coincidence of crossing Fifth Avenue during a parade and hearing, from loudspeakers mounted on the South Asian Gay and Lesbian Association float, a song to which I had danced at my cousin's wedding. 5 10

In a subway car, my skin would typically fall in the middle of the color spectrum. On street corners, tourists would ask me for directions. I was, in four and a half years, never an American; I was *immediately* a New Yorker. What? My voice is rising? You are right; I tend to become sentimental when I think of that city. It still occupies a place of great fondness in my heart, which is quite something, I must say, given the circumstances under which, after only eight months of residence, I would later depart. 15 20

Certainly, much of my early excitement about New York was wrapped up in my excitement about Underwood Samson. I remember my sense of wonder on the day I reported for duty. Their offices were perched on the forty-first and forty-second floors of a building in midtown – higher than any two structures here in Lahore would be if they were stacked one atop the other – and while I had previously flown in airplanes and visited the Himalayas, nothing had prepared me for the drama, the *power* of the view from their lobby. This, I realized, was another world from Pakistan; supporting my feet were the achievements of the most technologically advanced civilization our species had ever known. 25 30

---

2 **dismount**: get off a horse or vehicle   8 **samosa**: Indian snack   **channa**: *Kichererbsen*   11 **float** (n): a large vehicle on which people in special costumes are carried in a festival   24 **perch on sth.**: be placed high up on sth.   30 **advanced**: having the most modern ideas, methods, etc.

Often, during my stay in your country, such comparisons troubled me. In fact, they did more than trouble me: they made me resentful. Four thousand years ago, we, the people of the Indus River basin, had cities that were laid out on grids and boasted
5 underground sewers, while the ancestors of those who would invade and colonize America were illiterate barbarians. Now our cities were largely unplanned, unsanitary affairs, and America had universities with individual endowments greater than our national budget for education. To be reminded of this vast disparity was, for me, to be
10 ashamed.

But not on that day. On that day, I did not think of myself as a Pakistani, but as an Underwood Samson trainee, and my firm's impressive offices made me *proud*. I wished I could show my parents and my brother! I stood still, taking in the vista, but not for long;
15 soon after our arrival we entering analysts were marched into a conference room for our orientation presentation. There a vice president by the name of Sherman – his head gleaming from a recent shave – laid out the ethos of our new outfit.

"We're a meritocracy," he said. "We believe in being the best. You
20 were the best candidates at the best schools in the country. That's what got you here. But meritocracy doesn't stop with recruiting. We'll rank you every six months. You'll know your rankings. Your bonuses and staffing will depend on them. If you do well, you'll be rewarded. If you don't, you'll be out the door. It's that simple. You'll
25 have your first rankings at the end of this training program."

Simple indeed. I glanced about me to see how my fellow trainees were responding. There were five of them, in addition to myself, and

---

3 **resentful**: feeling bitter or angry about sth.   3–4 **Indus River**: Pakistan's longest river   4 **basin** ['beɪsən]: *Flussbecken*   **grid**: a pattern of straight lines, usually crossing each other to form squares   4 **boast sth.**: have sth. that is impressive
5 **sewer** ['suːər]: an underground pipe that is used to carry waste water away from a city   6 **illiterate**: unable to read   7 **unsanitary**: unclean   8 **endowment**: money given to an institution   9 **disparity**: imbalance, difference between two things
12 **trainee**: *Auszubildende/r*   14 **vista**: a beautiful view   17 **gleam**: shine
18 **ethos** ['iːθɑːs]: the moral ideas and attitudes of a particular group or society
23 **bonus**: an extra amount of money that is added to a payment as a reward
staffing: *Personalausstattung*

four sat rigidly at attention; the fifth, a chap called Wainwright, was more relaxed. Twirling his pen between his fingers in a fashion reminiscent of Val Kilmer in *Top Gun,* he leaned towards me and whispered, "No points for second place, Maverick." "You're dangerous, Ice Man," I replied – attempting to approximate a naval   5
aviator's drawl – and the two of us exchanged a grin.

But aside from light-hearted banter of this kind, there would be little in the way of fun and games at the workplace. For the next four weeks, our days followed a consistent routine. In the mornings we had a three-hour seminar: one of a series of modules that attempted   10
to abridge an entire year of business school. We were taught by professors from the most prestigious institutions – a Wharton woman, for example, instructed us in finance – and the results of the tests we were administered were carefully recorded.

Lunch was taken in the cafeteria; over chicken-pesto-in-sun-   15
dried-tomato wraps we observed the assured urgency with which our seniors conducted themselves. Afterwards we attended a workshop intended to familiarize us with computer programs such as PowerPoint, Excel, and Access. We spent this class sitting in a semicircle around a soft-spoken instructor who looked like a   20
librarian; Wainwright dubbed it our "Microsoft Family Time."

And finally, in the late afternoon we were divided into two teams of three for what Sherman referred to as "soft skills training." These sessions involved role-playing real-life situations, such as dealing with an irate client or an uncooperative chief financial officer. We   25
were taught to recognize another person's style of thought, harness their agenda, and redirect it to achieve our desired outcome; indeed one might describe it as a form of mental judo for business.

---

3 **reminiscent of sth.**: reminding you of sb./sth.   5 **approximate sth.**: imitate sth.
5–6 **naval aviator**: navy pilot   6 **drawl**: slow manner of speaking   7 **banter**:
friendly remarks and jokes   11 **abridge sth.**: shorten sth.   12 **Wharton School**:
oldest and one of the best business schools in the world   16 **assured**: confident
23 **soft skills**: personal attributes that help you be successful when interacting
with others in your job, e.g. communicative skills, opposite of "hard skills"
(e.g. intelligence, knowledge)   25 **irate** [aɪˈreɪt] (adj): very angry   26 **harness
sth.**: *sich etwas zunutze machen*

I see you are impressed by the thoroughness of our training. I was as well. It was a testament to the systematic pragmatism – call it *professionalism* – that underpins your country's success in so many fields. At Princeton, learning was imbued with an aura of creativity;
5   at Underwood Samson, creativity was not excised – it was still present and valued – but it ceded its primacy to *efficiency*. Maximum return was the maxim to which we returned, time and again. We learned to prioritize – to determine the axis on which advancement would be most beneficial – and then to apply ourselves single-
10   mindedly to the achievement of that objective.

But these musings of mine are perhaps rather dry! I do not mean to imply that I did not enjoy my initiation to the realm of high finance. On the contrary, I did. I felt empowered, and besides, all manner of new possibilities were opening up to me. I will give you
15   an example: expense accounts. Do you know how exhilarating it is to be issued a credit card and told that your company will pick up the tab for any ostensibly work-related meal or entertainment? Forgive me: of course you do; you are here, after all, on business. But for me, at the age of twenty-two, this experience was a revelation.
20   I could, if I desired, take my colleagues out for an after-work drink – an activity classified as "new hire cultivation" – and with impunity spend in an hour more than my father earned in a day!

As you can imagine, we new hires availed ourselves of the opportunity to cultivate one another on a regular basis. I remember
25   the first night we did so; we went to the bar at the Royalton, on Forty-Fourth Street. Sherman came with us on this occasion and ordered a bottle of vintage champagne to celebrate our induction.

---

3 **underpin sth.**: support sth.   4 **imbue sth. with sth.** (fml): fill sth. with sth. (e.g. emotions, values)   5 **excise sth.** (fml): remove sth. completely   6 **cede sth.**: give sth. up, usu. unwillingly   **primacy** ['praɪməsi]: position as most important thing   6–7 **maximum return**: *maximaler Ertrag*   7 **maxim**: (here) idea or rule that determines people's behavior   8 **axis**: (here) course, way   10 **objective**: goal
11 **musings**: act of telling sb. about your thoughts   12 **realm** [relm]: area of activity
13 **empowered** (adj): having strength and power   15 **expense account**:
Spesenkonto   17 **tab**: (*in einer Bar oder einem Restaurant*) *Rechnung*   **ostensible**:
vorgeblich   21 **with impunity**: *straffrei*   23 **avail yourself of sth.**: make use of sth.
27 **vintage**: (of wine and champagne) from a particularly good year

I looked around as we raised our glasses in a toast to ourselves. Two of my five colleagues were women; Wainwright and I were non-white. We were marvelously diverse … and yet we were not: all of us, Sherman included, hailed from the same elite universities – Harvard, Princeton, Stanford, Yale; we all exuded a sense of confident self-satisfaction; and not one of us was either short or overweight. 5

It struck me then – no, I must be honest, it strikes me *now* – that shorn of hair and dressed in battle fatigues, we would have been virtually indistinguishable. Perhaps something similar had occurred to Wainwright, for he winked and said to me, rather presciently as it would turn out, "Beware the dark side, young Skywalker." He had a penchant for quoting lines from popular cinema, much as my mother quoted the poems of Faiz and Ghalib. But I suspect Wainwright made this particular allusion to *Star Wars* mostly in jest, for immediately afterwards he, like I – like all of us, for that matter – drank heartily. 10 15

Sherman left when the champagne was done, but he told us to continue to our hearts' content and to charge our bill to Underwood Samson. We did so, staggering out into the street around midnight. Wainwright and I shared a cab downtown. "Hey man," he said, "do you *get* cricket?" I asked him what he meant. "My dad's nuts about it," he said. "He's from Barbados. West Indies versus Pakistan" – and here he slipped into a Caribbean lilt – "best damn test match I ever saw." I laughed. "That must have been in the eighties," I said. "Neither team is quite so good now." 20 25

We were both hungry, and I suggested we stop at the Pak-Punjab Deli. The man behind the counter recognized me; he had given me a free meal that morning when I mentioned it was my first day of work. "My friend," he said, spreading his arms in welcome. "Jenaab," I replied, bowing my head, "do you never go home?" "Not enough," 30

---

5 **exude sth.**: *etwas verströmen/ausstrahlen*   7 **strike sb.**: come into sb.'s mind
8 **shorn**: cut off   **battle fatigues**: loose clothes worn by soldiers in a fight
9 **indistinguishable**: looking all the same   10 **prescient** ['presiənt]: knowing or appearing to know about things before they happen   11–12 **have a penchant for sth.**: have a special liking for sth.   14 **allusion to sb./sth.**: reference to sb./sth.
in jest: as a joke   23 **lilt**: *Tonfall*   **test match**: cricket match between two nations which usually lasts several days

he said. "This time I insist on paying," I told him, unsheathing my credit card and leaning forward – both conspiratorially and drunkenly – to add, "I have an expense account." He shook his head and informed me, to the visible amusement of the exhausted
5   cabdrivers present, that he was sorry, and I could always pay later if I did not have the money, but he did not accept American Express.

Although we were speaking in Urdu, Wainwright seemed to understand. "I have cash," he said. "This stuff looks delicious." I was pleased he thought so; our food, as you have surely gathered in your
10 time here, is something we Lahoris take great pride in. Moreover, it is a mark of friendship when someone treats you to a meal – ushering you thereby into a relationship of mutual generosity – and by the time fifteen minutes later that I saw Wainwright licking his fingers, having dispatched the last crumb on his plate, I knew I had found a
15 kindred spirit at the office.

But why do you recoil? Ah yes, this beggar is a particularly unfortunate fellow. One can only wonder what series of *accidents* could have left him so thoroughly disfigured. He draws close to you because you are a foreigner. Will you give him something? No? Very
20 wise; one ought not to encourage beggars, and yes, you are right, it is far better to donate to charities that address the causes of poverty rather than to him, a creature who is merely its symptom. What am I doing? I am handing him a few rupees – misguidedly, of course, and out of habit. There, he offers us his prayers for our well-being;
25 now he is on his way.

I was telling you about Wainwright. Over the following weeks, it became clear that he was in strong contention for the top position in our rankings. All of us analyst trainees were competitive by nature – we had to have been for us to have acquired the grades necessary for
30 consideration by Underwood Samson – but Wainwright was less

---

1 **unsheath sth.**: take sth. (usu. a sword or knife) out of its cover   2 **conspiratorial**: suggesting that a secret is being shared   11 **mark**: sign   11–12 **usher sb. into sth.**: introduce sb. into sth.   16 **recoil**: move quickly away from sb./sth. frightening
18 **disfigure sb./sth.**: *jdn./etwas entstellen*   23 **misguided**: inappropriate, because of wrong judgement   27 **in contention for sth.** (fml): with a chance of winning sth.
28 **competitive**: trying very hard to be better than others

overtly so; he was genial and irreverent, and was as a consequence almost universally well-liked. But there was no doubt in my mind that my friend was also extremely talented: his presentations were remarkably clear; he excelled in our interpersonal exercises; and he had an instinct for identifying what mattered most in a business   5 case.

I hope you will not think me immodest when I say that I, too, stood out from the pack. I retained from my soccer-playing days a sort of controlled aggression – not belligerence, mind you, but determination – and I harnessed this to my desire to succeed. How   10 so? Well, I worked hard – harder, I suspect, than any of the others: subsisting on only a few hours of sleep a night – and I approached every class with utter concentration. My tenacity was frequently commented upon, with approval, by our instructors. Moreover, my natural politeness and sense of formality, which had sometimes been   15 a barrier in my dealings with my peers, proved perfectly suited to the work context in which I now found myself.

I have subsequently wondered why my mannerisms so appealed to my senior colleagues. Perhaps it was my speech: like Pakistan, America is, after all, a former English colony, and it stands to reason,   20 therefore, that an Anglicized accent may in your country continue to be associated with wealth and power, just as it is in mine. Or perhaps it was my ability to function both respectfully and with self-respect in a hierarchical environment, something American youngsters – unlike their Pakistani counterparts – rarely seem trained to do.   25 Whatever the reason, I was aware of an advantage conferred upon me by my foreignness, and I tried to utilize it as much as I could.

My high estimation of Wainwright's and my performance was confirmed when we trainees were divided into two groups of three for our drive to the annual summer party. One group, including   30 Wainwright and me, rode in a limousine with Jim, the managing

---

1 **overt** (fml): done in an open way and not secretly   **genial** ['dʒiːniəl]: friendly and cheerful   **irreverent**: not showing respect to sb./sth. who/that is usually respected
4 **excel**: do extremely well   9 **belligerence**: hostility, aggressiveness   12 **subsist on sth.**: live on sth.   13 **tenacity**: determination, persistence   16 **peer**: a person of the same age or social status   26 **confer sth. on sb.** (fml): give sb. sth. (e.g. a particular honour or right)

director who had hired us; the other group rode with Sherman, who, as a vice president, was more junior in the Underwood Samson pantheon. Since nothing at our firm happened by chance, we all knew this was a sign.

5   With us in the limousine were some associates and a vice president from one of Jim's teams. Everyone began to chat – everyone, that is, except Jim and myself. Jim observed the conversation in silence. Then he glanced in my direction, and I had to avert my eyes so he did not catch *me* observing *him*. But he
10   continued to look at me in his steady, penetrating manner until eventually he said, "You're a watchful guy. You know where that comes from?" I shook my head. "It comes from feeling out of place," he said. "Believe me. I know."

The party was being held at Jim's house in the Hamptons, a
15   magnificent property that made me think of *The Great Gatsby*. It was beside the beach – on a rise behind a protective ridge of sand dunes – and it had a swimming pool, a tennis court, and an open-sided white pavilion erected at one end of the lawn for drinking and dancing. A swing band struck up as we arrived, and I could smell steak and
20   lobster being thrown on a grill. Wainwright seemed very much in his element: he took one of the associates by the arm and soon they were twirling to the beat of the music. The rest of us watched from the sidelines, cocktails in hand.

After a while, I stepped outside the pavilion for some air. The sun
25   had set, and I could see the lights of other houses twinkling in the distance along the curve of the shore. The waves were whispering as they came in, causing me to recall being in Greece not long ago. The sea had always seemed far away to me, luxurious and full of adventure; now it was becoming almost a regular part of my life.
30   How much had changed in the four years since I had left Lahore!

---

3 **pantheon** (fml): a group of famous or important people   5 **associate** (n): (here) high-ranking business colleague   10 **penetrating** (adj): making you feel uncomfortable because the person seems to know what you are thinking
15 **The Great Gatsby**: novel (1932) by F. Scott Fitzgerald about a wealthy yet mysterious man   19 **strike up**: begin to play music   22 **twirl**: move or dance round and round

"I remember my first Underwood Samson summer party," a voice said behind me. I turned; it was Jim. He continued, "It was a gorgeous evening, like this one. Barbecue going, music playing. Reminded me of Princeton for some reason, of how I felt when I got there. I figured, I wouldn't mind having a place out in the Hamptons 5 myself one day." I smiled; Jim made one feel he could hear one's thoughts. "I know what you mean," I said. Jim let his gaze wander out over the water, and for a time we stood together in silence. Then he said, "You hungry?" "Yes," I replied. "Good," he said approvingly, and with that he tapped me on either shoulder with the blade of his 10 hand – an odd, deliberate gesture – and led me back inside.

I found myself wishing during the course of the evening that Erica were there. You wondered what had become of her? No, I had not forgotten; she was very much a part of my life in New York, and I shall return to her shortly. For the moment, though, I wanted only 15 to mention in passing that Jim's house was so splendid, I thought even *she* might be impressed. And that, as you will come to understand, is saying a great deal.

A week later, when the analyst training program came to an end, Jim called us one by one to his office. "So," he asked me, "how do 20 you think you did?" "Fairly well," I replied. He laughed. "You did better than fairly well," he said. "You're number one in your class. Your instructors say you've got a bit of the warrior in you. Don't be ashamed of that. Nurture it. It can take you a long way." I was enormously pleased, but I did not know what to say. "I've got a 25 project coming up," Jim went on. "Music business. Philippines. Want to be on it?" "I certainly do," I said. "Thank you."

When I left Jim's office, I found Wainwright waiting for me. "I came second this time," he said, smiling. "I figured you'd be first. And by the way you're glowing, I can see I was right." "I got lucky," 30

3 **gorgeous**: very beautiful and attractive   16 **in passing**: done or said while you are giving your attention to sth. else   16 **splendid**: impressive, beautiful
23 **warrior**: a person who fights in a battle or war   24 **nurture sth.**: help sth. to develop and be successful   29 **figure**: think   30 **glow**: have a feeling of pleasure and satisfaction

I replied. "Not that lucky," he said, putting his arm around my shoulders. "You've got to buy me a drink."

Yes, I was happy in that moment. I felt bathed in a warm sense of accomplishment. Nothing troubled me; I was a young New Yorker
5 with the city at my feet. How soon that would change! My world would be transformed, just as this market around us has been. See how quickly they have brought those tables into the street. Crowds have begun to stroll where only a few minutes ago there was the rumble of traffic. Coming upon this scene now, one might think that
10 Old Anarkali looked *always* thus, regardless of the hour. But we, sir, who have been sitting here for some time, we know better, do we not? Yes, we have acquired a certain familiarity with the recent history of our surroundings, and that – in my humble opinion – allows us to put the present into much better perspective.

---

3 **sense**: feeling   4 **accomplishment**: achievement   10 **regardless of sth.**: without being affected or influenced by sth.   13 **humble**: *bescheiden*

4

I see that you have noticed the scar on my forearm, here, where the skin is both darker and smoother than that which surrounds it. I have been told that it looks like a rope burn; my more active friends say it is not dissimilar to marks on the bodies of those who have taken up rappelling – or mountain climbing, for that matter. Perhaps 5 a thought of this nature is passing through *your* mind, for I detect a certain seriousness in your expression, as though you are wondering what sort of training camp could have given a fellow from the plains such as myself cause to engage in these activities!

Allow me, then, to reassure you that the source of my injury was 10 rather prosaic. We have in this country a phenomenon with which you will doubtless be unfamiliar, given the state of plenty that characterizes your homeland. Here – particularly in the winter, when the reservoirs of the great dams are almost dry – we face a shortage of electricity that manifests itself in rolling blackouts. We 15 call this load-shedding, and we keep our homes well-stocked with candles so that it does not unduly disrupt our lives. As a child, during such a time of load-shedding, I grabbed hold of one of these candles, tipped it over, and spilled molten wax on myself. In America, this would have been the start, in all likelihood, of a 20 protracted bout of litigation with the manufacturer for using candle-wax with such a high, and unsafe, melting point; here, it resulted merely in an evening of crying and the rather faint, if oddly linear, scar you see today.

---

5 **rapelling** [ræ'pelɪŋ]: *Abseilen*   11 **prosaic** [proʊ'zeɪɪk]: dull, not romantic
12 **plenty** (n, fml): a situation in which there is a large supply of food, money, etc.
15 **manifest sth.**: show sth.   **rolling blackout**: stopping the supply of electricity for a period of time in different geographical regions due to the demand being greater than the supply   19 **molten**: melted   20 **in all likelihood**: very probably
21 **protracted**: lasting longer than expected   **bout** [baʊt]: a short period of great activity   **litigation**: *Rechtsstreit*

Ah, they have begun to turn on the decorative lights that arc through the air above this market! A little gaudy? Yes, you are right; I myself might have chosen something less colorful. But observe the smiles on the upturned faces of those around us. It is remarkable
5 how *theatrical* manmade light can be once sunlight has begun to fade, how it can affect us emotionally, even now, at the start of the twenty-first century, in cities as large and bright as this one. Think of the expressive beauty of the Empire State Building, illuminated green for St. Patrick's Day, or pale blue on the evening of Frank
10 Sinatra's death. Surely, New York by night must be one of the greatest sights in the world.

I remember my early nocturnal explorations of Manhattan, so often with Erica as my guide. She invited me to her home for dinner soon after our return from Greece; I spent the afternoon deciding
15 what to wear. I knew her family was wealthy, and I wanted to dress as I imagined they would be dressed: in a manner elegant but also casual. My suit seemed too formal; my blazer would have been better, but it was several years old and struck me as somewhat shabby. In the end, I took advantage of the ethnic exception clause
20 that is written into every code of etiquette and wore a starched white kurta of delicately worked cotton over a pair of jeans.

It was a testament to the open-mindedness and – that overused word – *cosmopolitan* nature of New York in those days that I felt completely comfortable on the subway in this attire. Indeed, no one
25 seemed to take much notice of me at all, save for a gay gentleman who politely offered me an invitational smile. I emerged from the 6 train onto Seventy-Seventh Street, in the heart of the Upper East Side. The area – with its charming bistros, exclusive shops, and attractive women in short skirts walking tiny dogs – felt surprisingly
30 familiar, although I had never been there before; I realized later that

---

2 **gaudy**: too brightly coloured in a way that lacks taste   12 **nocturnal**: nightly
19 **shabby**: in a bad state   **ethnic exception clause**: attitude that people in your
own group but who come from a different culture can behave differently (**clause**:
Klausel)   21 **kurta**: a loose shirt, worn by men or women in southern Asia
22 **testament**: piece of evidence, proof   24 **attire**: clothes   27–28 **Upper East
Side**: wealthy area in Manhattan

I owed my sense of familiarity to the many films that had used it as a setting.

Erica's family lived in an impressive building with a blue canopy and an elderly doorman, who adopted a coldly disapproving expression that would not have been out of place on the face of the 5 gatekeeper of one of Lahore's larger mansions had I driven up in a small and rusted automobile. Naturally, I responded with an equally cold and rather imperious tone – carefully calibrated to convey both that I had taken offense and that I found it beneath myself to say so – as I stated my business. This had its desired effect; he promptly rang 10 up to inquire whether I should be allowed to pass and – when informed that I should – directed me in person to the elevator. I was instructed to press the button for the penthouse, a term associated in my mind with luxury and – yes, I will confess – with pornography as well. So it was in a state of heightened expectation that I arrived at 15 the door of Erica's flat, which opened before I had a chance to knock.

Erica received me with a smile; her tanned skin seemed to glow with health. I had forgotten how stunning she was, and in that moment, pressed as we were into close proximity by the confines of the entryway, I was forced to lower my eyes. "Wow," she said, 20 reaching out to graze the embroidery on my kurta with the tip of her finger, "you look great." I responded that she did, too, which was true, although she was wearing a short Mighty Mouse T-shirt and did not appear to have been quite as preoccupied with issues of dress selection as I had been. She said she wanted to show me 25 something, and I followed her to her bedroom. It was roughly twice the size of my studio flat and contained cartons of university books, a desk with a computer and a laser printer, a massive bed covered with clothes, and a punching bag suspended from the ceiling on a

3 **canopy** (AE): a fabric covering supported on posts outside the entrance of a building that is   8 **imperious** [ɪmˈpɪriəs]: expecting people to obey you
calibrated (adj): measured   **convey sth.** (fml): *etwas (z:B. einen Eindruck) vermitteln*
18 **stunning**: extremely attractive or impressive   19 **proximity**: the state of being near sb./sth.   **confines** (pl): limits, borders   21 **graze sth.**: touch sth. lightly
24 **preoccupied with sb./sth.**: worrying continuously about sth. so that you do not pay attention to other things   29 **punching bag:** a heavy leather bag hung on a rope from the ceiling for boxing practice

chain; in short, it looked lived-in, the sort of room one has had one's entire life.

I felt a peculiar feeling; I felt at home. Perhaps it was because I had recently lived such a transitory existence – moving from one dorm room to the next – and longed for the settled nature of my past; perhaps it was because I missed my family and the comfort of a family residence, where generations stayed together, instead of apart in an atomized state of age segregation; or perhaps it was because a spacious bedroom in a prestigious apartment on the Upper East Side was, in American terms, the socioeconomic equivalent of a spacious bedroom in a prestigious house in Gulberg, such as the one in which I had grown up. Whatever the reason, it made me smile, and Erica, seeing me smile, smiled back and held up a slender, brown parcel.

"It's done," she said solemnly. I waited for her to say more, and when she did not, I asked, " 'It' being?" "My manuscript," she said. "I'm sending it to an agent tomorrow." I took it respectfully in both hands, resting it flat across my upturned palms. "Congratulations," I said, and then, noticing it was rather light, added, "Is this all of it?" She nodded. "It's more a novella than a novel," she said. "It leaves space for your thoughts to echo." I turned it over, appreciating the physicality of the package: the tape which sealed it, the dent in one corner. "Are you nervous?" I asked her. "I'm more unsettled than nervous," she said. "It's like I'm an oyster. I've had this sharp speck inside me for a long time, and I've been trying to make it more comfortable, so slowly I've turned it into a pearl. But now it's finally being taken out, and just as it's going I'm realizing there's a gap being left behind, you know, a dent on my belly where it used to sit. And so I kind of want to hold on to it for a little longer." "Why do you not, then?" I asked, returning it to her. "I already have," she said, and she smiled again. "It's been lying in this envelope since before we went to Greece."

---

4 **transitory** [ˌtrænsətəri]: moving around often and only staying in one place for a short time   5 **long for sb./sth.**: want sth. very much   7 **apart**: separate 8 **atomized**: reduced to atoms or very small pieces   9 **spacious**: having lots of space   14 **solemn** [ˈsɑːləm]: serious   19 **novella**: a short novel   21 **dent**: a hollow place in a hard surface, usu. caused by sth. hitting it   22 **unsettled**: not calm or relaxed   23 **oyster**: *Auster*   **speck**: a small spot

I was honored and pleased that she was confiding in me in this fashion. I met her eyes, and for the first time I perceived that there was something *broken* behind them, like a tiny crack in a diamond that becomes visible only when viewed through a magnifying lens; normally it is hidden by the brilliance of the stone. I wanted to know 5 what it was, what had caused her to create the pearl of which she had spoken. But I thought it would be presumptuous of me to ask; such things are revealed by a person when and to whom they choose. So I attempted to convey through my expression alone my desire to understand her and said nothing further. 10

As we were leaving her room, I noticed a sketch on the wall. It depicted under stormy skies a tropical island with a runway and a steep volcano; nestled in the caldera of the volcano was a lake with another, smaller island in it – an island on an island – wonderfully sheltered and calm. "What is this?" I asked. "Chris did it," she 15 replied, "when we were eight or nine. It's inspired by one of his Tintin comics, *Flight 714*." "It is beautiful," I said. She nodded. "Yeah," she said, "it is. His mother gave it to me when she was clearing out his stuff." I looked at it a moment longer, fascinated by the intricacy of the pencilwork. In its attention to detail – though 20 not, of course, in its style or subject – it reminded me of our miniature paintings, of the sort one would find if one ventured around the corner to the Lahore Museum or the National College of Arts.

Erica led me outside to their roof terrace – a private aerie with a 25 spectacular, eagle's-eye view of Manhattan – and introduced me to her parents. Her mother was sitting at a table-tennis table that had been converted with four place settings into the venue for our dinner; she held my hand, said hello, and then, still holding my hand, added approvingly to Erica, "Very nice." "Behave, Mom," Erica 30 replied. Her father stood at a grill, placing hamburgers onto plates; it

---

1 **confide in sb.**: tell sb. secrets as a sign of trust   2 **perceive sth.**: notice or become aware of sth.   7 **presumptuous** [prɪˈzʌmptʃuəs]: *anmaßend*   11 **sketch**: a simple drawing   12 **runway**: *Landebahn*   13 **caldera**: a very large hole in the top of a volcano   20 **intricacy** [ˈntrɪkəsi]: detailed complexity   25 **aerie** [ˈeri] (AE spelling): the nest of a bird of high on a rock   28 **venue** [ˈvenjuː]: a place where people meet for an organized event, e.g. a concert

was apparent from his demeanor that he was a man of consequence in the corporate world. As we took our seats for the meal, he lifted a bottle of red wine and said to me, "You drink?" "He's twenty-two," Erica's mother said on my behalf, in a tone that suggested, *So of*
5 *course he drinks.* "I had a Pakistani working for me once," Erica's father said. "Never drank." "I do, sir," I assured him. "Thank you."

You seem puzzled by this – and not for the first time. Perhaps you misconstrue the significance of my beard, which, I should in any case make clear, I had not yet kept when I arrived in New York. In
10 truth, many Pakistanis drink; alcohol's illegality in our country has roughly the same effect as marijuana's in yours. Moreover, not all of our drinkers are western-educated urbanites such as myself; our newspapers regularly carry accounts of villagers dying or going blind after consuming poor-quality moonshine. Indeed, in our poetry and
15 folk songs *intoxication* occupies a recurring role as a facilitator of love and spiritual enlightenment. What? Is it not a sin? Yes, it certainly is – and so, for that matter, is coveting thy neighbor's wife. I see you smile; we understand one another, then.

But I digress. I was telling you of my first meal with Erica's family.
20 It was a warm evening, like this one – summer in New York being like spring here in Lahore. A breeze was blowing then, again as it is now, and it carried a smell of flame-cooked meat not dissimilar to that coming to us from the many open-air restaurants in this market that are beginning their preparations for dinner. The setting was
25 superb, the wine was delicious, the burgers were succulent, and our conversation was for the most part rather pleasant. Erica seemed happy that I was there, and her happiness infected me as well.

I do, however, remember becoming annoyed at one point in the discussion. Erica's father had asked me how things were back home,

---

1 **demeanor** [di'mi:nər]: the way that sb. looks or behaves   **consequence** (fml): importance   4 **on sb.'s behalf**: in sb.'s name   8 **misconstrue**: misinterpret, misunderstand   12 **urbanite** ['ɜ:rbənaɪt]: a person who lives in a town or city   13 **account** (n): report   14 **moonshine** (AE, old-fashioned): strong alcoholic drinks made and sold illegally   15 **intoxication**: state of being drunk   **recurring** [ri'kɜ:rɪŋ] (adj): happening often   17 **covet sb./sth.** (fml): want sb./sth. very much   19 **digress**: start to talk about sth. that is not connected with the main point of what you are saying   25 **succulent** ['sʌkjələnt]: juicy

and I had replied that they were quite good, thank you, when he said, "Economy's falling apart though, no? Corruption, dictatorship, the rich living like princes while everyone else suffers. Solid people, don't get me wrong. I like Pakistanis. But the elite has raped that place well and good, right? And fundamentalism. You guys have got 5
some serious problems with fundamentalism."

I felt myself bridle. There was nothing overtly objectionable in what he had said; indeed, his was a summary with some knowledge, much like the short news items on the front page of *The Wall Street Journal,* which I had recently begun to read. But his tone – with, if 10
you will forgive me, its typically *American* undercurrent of condescension – struck a negative chord with me, and it was only out of politeness that I limited my response to "Yes, there are challenges, sir, but my family is there, and I can assure you it is not as bad as that." 15

Fortunately, the remainder of our dinner passed without incident. Afterwards Erica and I shared a taxi down to Chelsea, where a friend of hers – the daughter of the owner of a contemporary art gallery – had invited her to a party to celebrate the opening of a show. I could hear our driver chatting on his mobile in Punjabi and knew from his 20
accent that he was Pakistani. Normally I would have said hello, but on that particular night I did not. Erica was watching me with considerable curiosity; eventually she remarked, "I hope you're not still upset about what my dad said." "Upset?" I responded. "Of course not. Not in the least." She laughed. "You're a terrible liar," she 25
said. "You're touchy about where you come from. It shows on your face." "Then I apologize," I said. "I had no right to be rude." "You're never rude," she said, smiling, "and I think it's good to be touchy sometimes. It means you care."

We alighted on West Twenty-Fourth Street. I insisted on paying 30
for our cab, and Erica led me by the hand into an unimpressive

---

4 **rape sth.**: rob sth., exploit sth.   7 **bridle** ['braɪdəl]: feel annoyed or offended at
sth.   11 **undercurrent**: undertone   12 **condescension** [ˌkɑːndɪ'senʃən]: behavior
that shows that you think you are more intelligent and important than sb. else
strike a chord with sb.: make sb. feel sth. deeply   16 **remainder**: rest
26 **touchy**: sensitive, easily upset or offended   30 **alight**: get out of a train, etc.

building, a decrepit, post-industrial hulk. Upon entering I heard music; it grew louder as we mounted several flights of stairs, until finally we pushed open a fire door and were immersed in sound. The gallery was a vast space, white, with clean lines and minimalist
5 fixtures; video projections of faces glowed on the blank heads of mannequins. I realized I was being ushered into an insider's world – the chic heart of this city – to which I would otherwise have had no access. We passed fashion models, old men with tans, artists in outrageous outfits; I was glad I had worn my kurta.

10 Erica was soon at the center of a circle of friends, none of whom I had previously met. I watched as she attracted people to her, and I was reminded of our trip to Greece, of the *gravity* she had exerted on our group. Yet this time was different; this time she had brought me with her, and she made certain – through a glance, the offer of a
15 drink, the touch of her hand at my elbow – that we remained connected throughout the evening. When she kissed me on the cheek hours later, as I held the door of the cab in which she would return to her home alone, I felt as though we had spent an intimate evening together, even though we had spoken little at the party.
20 Perhaps she felt the same, for at that very instant she said, "Thank you." I was taken by surprise; I thought I should be thanking her, but I had no time to say so, because she pulled the door shut and then she was gone.

In the weeks that followed, she did invite me to meet her on a
25 number of occasions. But unlike that first night – when we were together in her room and in the taxi – we were never again alone. We went to a small music venue on the Lower East Side, a French restaurant in the meatpacking district, a loft party in TriBeCa – but always in the company of others. Often, I found myself observing
30 Erica as she stood or sat, surrounded by her acquaintances. At these moments she frequently became introspective; it was as though their presence allowed her to withdraw, to recede a half-step inside

---

1 **decrepit**: very old and not in good condition   **hulk**: a very large object (here: building)   3 **immerse sb./sth.**: cover sb./sth. completely   20 **instant**: moment
27–28 **Lower East Side, the meatpacking district, TriBeCa**: trendy neighborhoods in Lower Manhattan   31 **become introspective**: *sich in sich selbst zurückziehen*

herself. She reminded me of a child who could sleep only with the door open and the light on.

Sometimes she would become aware of my gaze upon her, and then she would smile at me as though – or so I flattered myself to believe – I had placed a shawl around her shoulders as she returned 5 from a walk in the cold. We exchanged only pleasantries on these outings, and yet I felt our relationship was deepening. At the end of the evening she would kiss my cheek, and it seemed to me that she lingered a fraction longer each time, until her kisses lasted long enough for me to catch a trace of her scent and perceive the softness 10 of the indentation at the corner of her mouth.

My patience was rewarded the weekend before I left for Manila, when Erica asked me to join her for a picnic lunch in Central Park and I discovered that we were not to be met by anyone else. It was one of those glorious late-July afternoons in New York when a stiff 15 wind off the Atlantic makes the trees swell and the clouds race across the sky. You know them well? Yes, precisely: the humidity vanishes as the city fills its lungs with cooler, briny air. Erica wore a straw hat and carried a wicker basket containing wine, fresh-baked bread, sliced meats, several different cheeses, and grapes – a delicious and, 20 to my mind, rather sophisticated assortment.

We chatted as we ate, lounging in the grass. "Do people have picnics in Lahore?" she asked me. "Not so much in the summer," I told her. "At least not if they have any choice in the matter. The sun is too strong, and the only people one sees sitting outside are 25 clustered in the shade." "So this must seem very foreign to you, then," she said. "No," I replied, "in fact it reminds me of when my family would go up to Nathia Galli, in the foothills of the Himalayas. There we often used to take our meals in the open – with tea and cucumber sandwiches from the hotel." She smiled at the image, then 30 became thoughtful and fell silent.

---

6 **pleasantry**: a friendly remark made in order to be polite   9 **linger**: stay close to sb./sth. even when you don't have to   **fraction**: a small part or amount of sth.
16 **swell**: become bigger or rounder   17 **humidity**: the amount of water in the air
22 **lounge** (v): stand, sit or lie in a lazy way   28 **Nathia Galli**: a mountain resort town in Pakistan

"I haven't done this in a long time," she told me when she spoke again. "Chris and I used to come to the park a lot. We'd bring this basket with us and just read or hang out for hours." "Was it when he died," I asked, "that you stopped coming?" "I stopped," she answered,
5 plucking a daisy, "a bunch of things. For a while I stopped talking to people. I stopped eating. I had to go to the hospital. They told me not to think about it so much and put me on medication. My mom had to take three months off work because I couldn't be by myself. We kept it quiet, though, and by September I was back at Princeton."
10 That was all she said, and she said it in a normal, if quiet, voice. But I glimpsed again – even more clearly than before – the crack inside her; it evoked in me an almost familial tenderness. When we got up to depart, I offered her my arm and she smiled as she accepted it. Then the two of us walked off, leaving Central Park behind.
15 I remember vividly the feeling of her skin, cool and smooth, on mine. We had never before remained in contact for such a prolonged period; the sensation that her body was so strong and yet belonged to someone so wounded lingered with me until long afterwards. Indeed, weeks later, in my hotel room in Manila, I would at times
20 wake up to that sensation as though touched by a ghost.

What bad luck! The lights have gone. But why do you leap to your feet? Do not be alarmed, sir; as I mentioned before, fluctuations and blackouts are common in Pakistan. Really, you are overreacting; it is not yet so dark. The sky above us still contains a tinge of color,
25 and I can see you quite clearly as you stand there with your hand in your jacket. I assure you: no one will attempt to steal your wallet. For a city of this size, Lahore is remarkably free of that sort of petty crime. Do sit down, I implore you, or you shall force me to stand as well. As it is, I feel rude to remain in this position while my guest is
30 uncomfortable.

Ah, they are back! Thank goodness. It was nothing more than a momentary disruption. And you – to jump as though you were a

---

5 **pluck sth.**: pick sth.   **daisy**: *Gänseblümchen*   11 **crack**: *Riss*   12 **evoke sth.**: create a feeling of sth.   15 **vivid**: intense   21 **leap**: jump up suddenly and quickly 27–28 **petty crime**: small crime (e.g. stealing)   28 **implore sb.** (fml): beg sb., ask sb. earnestly

mouse suddenly under the shadow of a hawk! I would offer you a whiskey to settle your nerves, if only I could. A Jack Daniels, eh? You smile; I have hit upon a spirit to which you are partial. Sadly, all the beverages in this market that can trace their origin to your country are carbonated soft drinks. One of those will do? Then I will summon ₅ our waiter immediately.

---

3 **partial to sb./sth.** (old-fashioned): liking sb./sth. very much   4 **beverage** ['bevərɪdʒ]: drink   5 **carbonated**: containing small bubbles of carbon dioxide **soft drink**: a non-alcoholic drink   **summon sb.** (fml): call sb.

5

Observe, sir: bats have begun to appear in the air above this square. Creepy, you say? What a delightfully American expression – one I have not heard in many years! I do not find them creepy; indeed, I quite like them. They remind me of when I was younger; they would
5 swoop at us as we swam in my grandfather's pool, perhaps mistaking us for frogs. Lahore was home to even larger creatures of the night back then – flying foxes, my father used to call them – and when we drove along Mall Road in the evenings we would see them hanging upside down from the canopies of the oldest trees. They are gone
10 now; it is possible that, like butterflies and fireflies, they belonged to a *dreamier* world incompatible with the pollution and congestion of a modern metropolis. Today, one glimpses them only in the surrounding countryside.

But bats have survived here. They are successful urban dwellers,
15 like you and I, swift enough to escape detection and canny enough to hunt among a crowd. I marvel at their ability to navigate the cityscape; no matter how close they come to these buildings, they are never involved in a collision. Butterflies, on the other hand, tend to splatter on the windshields of passing automobiles, and I have
20 once seen a firefly bumping repeatedly against the window of a house, unable to comprehend the glass that barred its way. Maybe flying foxes lacked the radar – or the agility – of their smaller cousins and therefore hurtled to their deaths against Lahore's newer offices and plazas – structures that rose higher than any had before. If so,

---

2 **creepy** (infml): scary, spooky   5 **swoop at sb./sth.**: fly quickly and suddenly downwards towards sb./sth.   7 **flying fox**: *Flughund*   8 **Mall Road**: one of Lahore´s main roads, known for its historic buildings   10 **firefly**: *Glühwürmchen*
11 **incompatible**: impossible to be mixed together   14 **urban dweller**: a person that lives in a city   15 **swift**: fast, quick   **canny**: intelligent, careful   16 **marvel at sth.**: be very surprised or impressed by sth.   21 **bar sth.**: block sth.   23 **hurtle**: move very fast in a particular direction

they would have long been extinct in New York – or even in Manila, for that matter!

When I arrived in the Philippines at the start of my first Underwood Samson assignment, I was terribly excited. We had flown first-class, and I will never forget the feeling of reclining in my   5
seat, clad in my suit, as I was served champagne by an attractive and – yes, I was indeed so brazen as to allow myself to believe – *flirtatious* flight attendant. I was, in my own eyes, a veritable James Bond – only younger, darker, and possibly better paid. How odd it seems now to recall that time; how quickly my sense of self-   10
satisfaction would later disappear!

But I am getting ahead of myself. I was telling you about Manila. Have you been to the East, sir? You have! Truly, you are well-traveled for an American – for a person of any country, for that matter. I am increasingly curious as to the nature of your *business* – but I am   15
certain you will tell me in due course; for the moment you seem to prefer that I continue. Since you have been to the East, you do not need me to explain how prodigious are the changes taking place in that part of the globe. I expected to find a city like Lahore – or perhaps Karachi; what I found instead was a place of skyscrapers   20
and superhighways. Yes, Manila had its slums; one saw them on the drive from the airport: vast districts of men in dirty white undershirts lounging idly in front of auto-repair shops – like a poorer version of the 1950s America depicted in such films as *Grease*. But Manila's glittering skyline and walled enclaves for the ultra-rich were unlike   25
anything I had seen in Pakistan.

I tried not to dwell on the comparison; it was one thing to accept that New York was more wealthy than Lahore, but quite another to swallow the fact that Manila was as well. I felt like a distance runner who thinks he is not doing too badly until he glances over his   30
shoulder and sees that the fellow who is lapping him is not the

---

1 **extinct**: no longer in existence   **Manila**: capital of the Philippines
4 **assignment**: task, mission   7 **brazen** ['breɪzən]: shameless   18 **prodigious** [prə'dɪdʒəs]: colossal, enormous   20 **Karachi**: largest city of Pakistan   25 **walled enclave** ['enkleɪv]: gated community, in which wealthy residents are separated by fences and security measures from the area around it   27 **dwell on sth.**: think or talk a lot about sth.   31 **lap sb.**: *jdn. überrunden*

leader of the pack, but one of the laggards. Perhaps it was for this reason that I did something in Manila I had never done before: I attempted to act and speak, as much as my dignity would permit, more like an American. The Filipinos we worked with seemed to
5   look up to my American colleagues, accepting them almost instinctively as members of the officer class of global business – and I wanted my share of that respect as well.

So I learned to tell executives my father's age, "I need it *now*"; I learned to cut to the front of lines with an extraterritorial smile;
10   and I learned to answer, when asked where I was from, that I was from New York. Did these things trouble me, you ask? Certainly, sir; I was often ashamed. But outwardly I gave no sign of this. In any case, there was much for me to be proud of: my genuine aptitude for our work, for example, and the glowing reviews my performance
15   received from my peers.

We were there, as I mentioned to you earlier, to value a recorded-music business. The owner had been a legendary figure in the local A&R scene; when he removed his sunglasses, his eyes contained the sort of cosmic openness one associates with prolonged exposure to
20   LSD. But despite his colorful past, he had managed to sign lucrative outsourcing deals to manufacture and distribute CDs for two of the international music majors. Indeed, he claimed his operation was the largest of its kind in Southeast Asia and – piracy, downloads, and Chinese competition notwithstanding – growing at quite a healthy
25   clip.

To determine how much it was actually worth, we worked around the clock for over a month. We interviewed suppliers, employees, and experts of all kinds; we passed hours in closed rooms with accountants and lawyers; we gathered gigabytes of data; we

---

1 **laggard** ['lægərd] (old-fashioned): a slow and lazy person   8 **executive** [ɪg'zekjətɪv]: manager   9 **extraterritorial**: showing that you are foreign and are entitled to certain privileges   18 **A&R = artists and repertoire**:the division of a record company that is responsible for discovering new artists   20 **LSD**: hallucinatory drug   **lucrative** ['lu:krətɪv]: profitable   21 **outsourcing**: moving parts of a company to other countries in order to cut costs   24 **notwithstanding** (fml): despite this   24–25 **at a healthy clip**: quickly   29 **accountant**: *Buchhalter/in*

compared indicators of performance to benchmarks; and, in the end, we built a complex financial model with innumerable permutations. I spent much of my time in front of my computer, but I also visited the factory floor and several music shops. I felt enormously powerful on these outings, knowing my team was 5 shaping the future. Would these workers be fired? Would these CDs be made elsewhere? *We,* indirectly of course, would help decide.

Yet there were moments when I became disoriented. I remember one such occasion in particular. I was riding with my colleagues in a limousine. We were mired in traffic, unable to move, and I glanced 10 out the window to see, only a few feet away, the driver of a jeepney returning my gaze. There was an undisguised hostility in his expression; I had no idea why. We had not met before – of that I was virtually certain – and in a few minutes we would probably never see one another again. But his dislike was so obvious, so *intimate,* that it 15 got under my skin. I stared back at him, getting angry myself – you will have noticed in your time here that glaring is something we men of Lahore take seriously – and I maintained eye contact until he was obliged by the movement of the car in front to return his attention to the road. 20

Afterwards, I tried to understand why he acted as he did. Perhaps, I thought, his wife has just left him; perhaps he resents me for the privileges implied by my suit and expensive car; perhaps he simply does not like Americans. I remained preoccupied with this matter far longer than I should have, pursuing several possibilities that all 25 assumed – as their unconscious starting point – that he and I shared a sort of Third World sensibility. Then one of my colleagues asked me a question, and when I turned to answer him, something rather strange took place. I looked at him – at his fair hair and light eyes and, most of all, his oblivious immersion in the minutiae of our 30

---

1 **benchmark**: *Bezugsgröße, Vergleichsindex*   2 **innumerable** [ɪ'nju:mərəbl]: too many to be counted   3 **permutation**: possible variation   10 **mired in sth.**(fml): stuck in sth. unpleasant that you cannot escape from   11 **jeepney**: a small Philippine bus converted from a jeep   12 **undisguised**: not hidden from other people, openly shown   **hostility**: unfriendly or aggressive feelings or behaviour 15 **intimate**: close and personal   30 **oblivious**: not aware of sth.   **minutiae** [maɪ'nu:ʃiaɪ] (pl): very small details

work – and thought, you are so *foreign*. I felt in that moment much
closer to the Filipino driver than to him; I felt I was play-acting when
in reality I ought to be making my way home, like the people on the
street outside.

5   I did not say anything, of course, but I was sufficiently unsettled
by this peculiar series of events – or impressions, really, for they
hardly constituted *events* – that I found it difficult to sleep that night.
Fortunately, however, the intensity of our assignment did not permit
me to indulge in further bouts of insomnia; the next day I was at the
10 office until two in the morning, and when I returned to my hotel
room, I slept like a baby.

    During my time in Manila – I arrived in late July and left in mid-
September – my main links to friends and family were weekly phone
calls to Lahore and online correspondence with Erica in New York.
15 Because of the time difference, messages she wrote in the morning
arrived in my inbox in the evening, and I looked forward to reading
and replying to them before I went to bed. Her emails were invariably
brief; she never wrote more than a paragraph or two. But she
managed to say a great deal with few words. One note, for example,
20 contained something to the effect of: "C. – I'm in the Hamptons.
A bunch of us were hanging out on the beach today and I went for a
walk by myself. I found this rock pool. Do you like rock pools?
I love them. They're like little worlds. Perfect, self-contained,
transparent. They look like they're frozen in time. Then the tide rises
25 and a wave crashes in and they start all over again with new fish left
behind. Anyway when I got back everyone kept asking where I'd
been and I realized I'd spent the entire afternoon there. It was kind
of surreal. Made me think of you. – E."

    Such messages were enough to lift my spirits for several days.
30 Perhaps this strikes you as an exaggeration. But you must understand
that in Lahore, at least when I was in secondary school – youngsters

---

5 **sufficiently**: enough for a particular purpose   7 **constitute sth.**: be the parts that
together form sth.   9 **indulge in sth.**: allow yourself to do sth. that you like, esp.
sth. that is considered bad for you   20 **the Hamptons**: a wealthy seaside resort for
New Yorkers on Long Island   24 **tide**: the flow of water as the sea rises and falls

here, like everywhere else, are probably more liberated now – relationships were often conducted over fleeting phone calls, messages through friends, and promises of encounters that never happened. Many parents were strict, and sometimes weeks would pass without us being able to meet those we thought of as our 5 girlfriends. So we learned to savor the denial of gratification – that most un-American of pleasures! – and I for one could subsist quite happily on a diet of emails such as that which I have just described.

But I was of course eager to see Erica again and was therefore in high spirits as our project approached its end. Jim had flown in to 10 satisfy himself with our final conclusions; he sat me down for a drink. "So, Changez," he said, taking in our exquisite hotel, the Makati ShangriLa, with a sweep of his hand, "getting used to all this?" "I am indeed, sir," I replied. "Everyone's saying great things about you," he said, pausing to see how I responded; when I smiled, 15 he went on, "Except that you're working too hard. You don't want to burn out, now." "Allow me to reassure you," I said. "I get more than enough rest." He raised an eyebrow and started to laugh. "I like you, you know that?" he said. "Really. Not in a bullshit, say-something-nice-to-raise-the-kid's-morale way. You're a shark. And that's a 20 compliment, coming from me. It's what they called me when I first joined. A shark. I never stopped swimming. And I was a cool customer. I never let on that I felt like I didn't belong to this world. Just like you."

It was not the first time Jim had spoken to me in this fashion; 25 I was always uncertain of how to respond. The confession that implicates its audience is – as we say in cricket – a devilishly difficult ball to play. Reject it and you slight the confessor; accept it and you admit your own guilt. So I said, rather carefully, "Why did you not belong?" He smiled – again as if he could see right through me – and 30

1 **liberated**: free from the restrictions of traditional ideas about social and sexual behavior   2 **fleeting** (adj): lasting only a short time   3 **encounter**: meeting 6 **savor sth.**: enjoy sth. thoroughly   **denial of sth.**: the refusal to allow sb. to have sth.   **gratification**: the state of feeling pleasure when sth. goes well   20 **morale** [məˈræl]: a person's amount of confidence and enthusiasm   27 **implicate sb.**: show or suggest that sb. is involved in sth. bad or criminal   28 **slight sb.**: treat sb. rudely or without respect

replied, "Because I grew up on the other side. For half my life, I was outside the candy store looking in, kid. And in America, no matter how poor you are, TV gives you a good view. But I was dirt poor. My dad died of gangrene. So I get the irony of paying a hundred bucks
5 for a bottle of fermented grape juice, if you know what I mean."

I thought about this. As I have already told you, I did not grow up in poverty. But I did grow up with a poor boy's sense of *longing,* in my case not for what my family had never had, but for what we had had and lost. Some of my relatives held on to imagined memories
10 the way homeless people hold onto lottery tickets. *Nostalgia* was their crack cocaine, if you will, and my childhood was littered with the consequences of their addiction: unserviceable debts, squabbles over inheritances, the odd alcoholic or suicide. In this, Jim and I were indeed similar: he had grown up outside the candy store, and I
15 had grown up on its threshold as its door was being shut.

We were joined at the bar by other members of the team, but Jim sat with his arm around the back of my chair in a way that made me feel – quite literally – as though he had taken me under his wing. It was a good feeling, and it felt even better when I saw how the hotel
20 staff was responding to him; they had identified Jim as a man of substance, and the smiles and attention he received were impressive to behold. I was the only non-American in our group, but I suspected my Pakistaniness was invisible, cloaked by my suit, by my expense account, and – most of all – by my companions.
25 And yet … No, I ought to pause here, for I think you will find rather unpalatable what I intend to say next, and I wish to warn you before I proceed. Besides, my throat is parched; the breeze seems to have disappeared entirely and, although night has fallen, it is still rather warm. Would you care for another soft drink? No? You are

---

2 **candy store** (AE): shop that sells sweets   4 **gangrene** [gæŋ'gri:n]: *Wundbrand*
5 **fermented grape juice**: (here) wine or champagne   11 **crack cocaine**: type of strong and addictive drug   12 **unserviceable**: that cannot be paid back on a regular basis   **squabble**: noisy argument, fight   13 **inheritance**: the money, property, etc. that you receive from sb. after they die   15 **threshold**: *Schwelle*   18 **take sb. under your wing**: *jdn. unter seine Fettiche nehmen*   23 **cloak sb./sth.**: hide/cover sb./ sth.   26 **unpalatable**: distasteful and not easy to accept   27 **proceed** (fml): continue talking   **parched**: very dry

curious, you say, and desire me to continue? Very well. I will just signal our waiter to bring a bottle for me; there, it is done. And here he comes, making such haste; one would think we were his only customers! Ah, delicious: this is precisely what I required.

The following evening was supposed to be our last in Manila. 5 I was in my room, packing my things. I turned on the television and saw what at first I took to be a film. But as I continued to watch, I realized that it was not fiction but news. I stared as one – and then the other – of the twin towers of New York's World Trade Center collapsed. And then I smiled. Yes, despicable as it may sound, my 10 initial reaction was to be remarkably pleased.

Your disgust is evident; indeed, your large hand has, perhaps without your noticing, clenched into a fist. But please believe me when I tell you that I am no sociopath; I am not indifferent to the suffering of others. When I hear of an acquaintance who has been 15 diagnosed with a serious illness, I feel – almost without fail – a sympathetic pain, a twinge in my kidneys strong enough to elicit a wince. When I am approached for a donation to charity, I tend to be forthcoming, at least insofar as my modest means will permit. So when I tell you I was pleased at the slaughter of thousands of 20 innocents, I do so with a profound sense of perplexity.

But at that moment, my thoughts were not with the *victims* of the attack – death on television moves me most when it is fictitious and happens to characters with whom I have built up relationships over multiple episodes – no, I was caught up in the symbolism of it all, the 25 fact that someone had so visibly brought America to her knees. Ah, I see I am only compounding your displeasure. I understand, of

---

10 **despicable** [di'spɪkəbəl]: *verabscheuungswürdig*   11 **initial**: first   12 **disgust**: a strong feeling of dislike or disapproval for sb./sth.   14 **sociopath** ['soʊsiopæθ]: a person who behaves in an aggressive or dangerous way towards other people **indifferent to sb./sth.**: not caring about sb./sth.   17 **twinge**: a sudden short feeling of pain   **kidney**: *Niere*   **elicit sth. from sb.** (fml): *jdm. etwas entlocken/hervorrufen* 18 **wince**: an expression on your face that shows that you are feeling pain or embarrassment   20 **slaughter**: the killing of large numbers of people at one time 21 **profound**: deeply/strongly felt   23 **fictitious**: *fiktiv*   25 **multiple**: many in number   27 **compound sth.**: make sth. bad become even worse

course; it is hateful to hear another person gloat over one's country's misfortune. But surely you cannot be completely innocent of such feelings yourself. Do you feel no joy at the video clips – so prevalent these days – of American munitions laying waste the structures of
5   your enemies?

But you are at war, you say? Yes, you have a point. I was not at war with America. Far from it: I was the product of an American university; I was earning a lucrative American salary; I was infatuated with an American woman. So why did part of me desire to see
10   America harmed? I did not know, then; I knew merely that my feelings would be unacceptable to my colleagues, and I undertook to hide them as well as I could. When my team gathered in Jim's room later that evening, I feigned the same shock and anguish I saw on the faces around me.

15   But hearing them speak of their loved ones, my thoughts turned to Erica, and I no longer needed to pretend. I did not yet know, of course, that the dying was confined to the limited geography of what would come to be called Ground Zero. Nor did I yet know that Erica was safely at home when the attacks took place. I was almost relieved
20   to be worried for her and unable to sleep; this allowed me to share in the anxiety of my colleagues and ignore for a time my initial sense of pleasure.

We were unable to leave Manila for several days, on account of flights being canceled. At the airport, I was escorted by armed guards
25   into a room where I was made to strip down to my boxer shorts – I had, rather embarrassingly, chosen to wear a pink pair patterned with teddy bears, but their revelation had no impact on the severe expressions of my inspectors – and I was, as a consequence, the last person to board our aircraft. My entrance elicited looks of concern
30   from many of my fellow passengers. I flew to New York uncomfortable

---

1 **gloat over sth.**: *sich an etwas weiden*   3 **prevalent**: common, widespread
8–9 **infatuated with sb./sth.** [ɪnˈfætʃueɪtəd]: having a very strong feeling of love or attraction for sb./sth. so that you cannot think clearly anymore   13 **feign sth.** [feɪn]: pretend that you have sth. (esp. a particular feeling)   **anguish**: suffering or unhappiness   18 **Ground Zero**: the former site of the World Trade Center
23 **on account of**: because of

in my own face: I was aware of being under suspicion; I felt guilty; I tried therefore to be as nonchalant as possible; this naturally led to my becoming stiff and self-conscious. Jim, who was sitting next to me, asked on multiple occasions if I was all right.

When we arrived, I was separated from my team at immigration. 5 They joined the queue for American citizens; I joined the one for foreigners. The officer who inspected my passport was a solidly built woman with a pistol at her hip and a mastery of English inferior to mine; I attempted to disarm her with a smile. "What is the purpose of your trip to the United States?" she asked me. "I live here," 10 I replied. "That is *not* what I asked you, sir," she said. "What is the *purpose* of your trip to the United States?" Our exchange continued in much this fashion for several minutes. In the end I was dispatched for a secondary inspection in a room where I sat on a metal bench next to a tattooed man in handcuffs. My team did not wait for me; by 15 the time I entered the customs hall they had already collected their suitcases and left. As a consequence, I rode to Manhattan that evening very much alone.

But why do you flinch? Ah yes, the bats; they are circling rather low. They will not touch us; allow me to reassure you on that score. 20 You know, you say? Your tone is curt; I can see that I have offended you, *angered* you even. But I have not, I suspect, entirely *surprised* you. Do you deny it? No? And *that* is of not inconsiderable interest to me, for we have not met before, and yet you seem to know at least something about me. Perhaps you have drawn certain conclusions 25 from my appearance, my lustrous beard; perhaps you have merely followed the arc of my tale with the uncanny skill of a skeet shooter; or perhaps ... But enough of these speculations! Let us cast our gaze over a menu; I have spoken too much, and I fear I have been negligent in my duties as a host. Besides, I wish now to hear more of 30 *you:* what brings you to Lahore, what company you work for, et

---

2 **nonchalant** [ˌnɑːnʃəˈlɑːnt]: behaving in a calm and relaxed way   9 **disarm sb.**: make sb. feel less angry or critical   13 **dispatch sb./sth.**: send sb./sth. in a particular direction   16 **customs**: *Zoll*   19 **flinch**: *zucken*   21 **curt**: appearing rude 26 **lustrous**: soft and shining   27 **skeet shooter**: *Tontaubenschießer/in* 30 **negligent** [ˈneɡlɪdʒənt]: failing to give sb./sth. enough care or attention

cetera, et cetera. Night is deepening around us, and despite the lights above this market, your face is mostly in shadow. Let us, like the bats, exercise our other senses, since our eyes are of diminishing utility. Your ears must be exhausted; the time has come to employ
5   your tongue – for taste, if nothing more, although I hope you can be persuaded to speak!

3 **diminishing**: decreasing   4 **utility**: usefulness

6

You hesitate, sir; I did not mean to put you on the spot. If you are not yet ready to reveal your *purpose* in traveling here – your demeanor all but precludes the possibility that you are a tourist wandering aimlessly through this part of the world – then I will not insist. Ah, I see that you have detected a scent. Nothing escapes you; 5 your senses are as acute as those of a fox in the wild. It is rather pleasant, is it not? Yes, you are right: it *is* jasmine. It comes, as your glance suggests you have already surmised, from the table beside ours, where that family has just taken their seats for dinner.

What a contrast: the paleness of those buds – strung with needle 10 and thread into a fluffy bracelet – against the darkness of that lady's skin! And what a contrast, again: the delicacy of their perfume against the robust smell of roasting meat! It is remarkable indeed how we human beings are capable of delighting in the mating call of a flower while we are surrounded by the charred carcasses of our 15 fellow animals – but then we are remarkable creatures. Perhaps it is in our nature to recognize subconsciously the link between mortality and procreation – between, that is to say, the finite and the infinite – and we are in fact driven by reminders of the one to seek out the other. 20

I remember being tasked with purchasing such flowers upon the death of my maternal grandmother. I was sixteen at the time and in possession of a fake motor vehicle learner's permit – it had been my brother's – and I was so excited to be behind the wheel of an automobile that I was regularly sent by my family to do errands that 25 might otherwise have been carried out by our chauffeur. Our Toyota

3 **preclude sth.**: make sth. impossible   6 **acute** [ə'kjuːt]: sharp   8 **surmise sth.**: guess or suppose sth. using the evidence you have   14 **mating call**: sound made by a male animal to attract females for sex   15 **charred**: turned black by fire   **carcass**: dead body   18 **procreation** (fml): act of producing children   23 **fake**: *gefälscht* 25 **errand** ['erənd]: a job that you do for sb. that involves going somewhere to take a message or to buy sth. or pick sth. up.

Corolla was lovingly maintained but getting on in years and therefore
prone – as happened in this particular case – to overheating. To this
day I can still recall the heady aroma of those strands of threaded
jasmine piled high in my arms as I walked to the cemetery, sweating
5   in the summer sun.

New York was in mourning after the destruction of the World
Trade Center, and floral motifs figured prominently in the shrines to
the dead and the missing that had sprung up in my absence. I would
often glance at them as I walked by: photos, bouquets, words of
10   condolence – nestled into street corners and between shops and
along the railings of public squares. They reminded me of my own
uncharitable – indeed, inhumane – response to the tragedy, and I felt
from them a constant murmur of reproach.

Other reproaches were far louder. Your country's flag invaded
15   New York after the attacks; it was everywhere. Small flags stuck on
toothpicks featured in the shrines; stickers of flags adorned
windshields and windows; large flags fluttered from buildings. They
all seemed to proclaim: *We are America* – not New York, which, in
my opinion, means something quite different – *the mightiest*
20   *civilization the world has ever known; you have slighted us; beware our*
wrath. Gazing up at the soaring towers of the city, I wondered what
manner of host would sally forth from so grand a castle.

It was against this backdrop that I saw Erica again. Six weeks had
passed since that afternoon we spent together in Central Park, and
25   when I called I thought Erica might have other plans, but she
suggested we meet that very evening, which is to say the evening of
my first full day back in New York, as soon as I was done with work.
I was waiting on the sidewalk as she stepped out of a taxi. A peculiar
odor lingered in the air; the smoldering wreckage downtown made
30   its way into our lungs. Her lips were pale, as though she had not
slept – or perhaps she had been crying. I thought in that moment

2 **prone to sth.**: likely to suffer from sth.   6 **mourning**: sadness that you show and
feel because sb. has died   10 **condolence**: *Anteilnahme*   13 **reproach**: blame or
criticism for sth. you have done   20 **slight sb.**: insult sb., treat sb. rudely or
without respect   21 **wrath [ræθ]** (fml): extreme anger   22 **sally forth** (old-
fashioned): leave a place   26 **very** (adj): same   29 **odor**: smell   **linger**: continue
to exist for longer than expected   **smolder**: burn slowly without a flame

that she looked older, more elegant; she had an element of that beauty which only age can confer upon a woman, and I imagined I was catching a glimpse of the Erica she would one day become. Truly, I thought, she is an empress-in-waiting!

"My mom was saying," she said over dinner, "maybe we should 5 leave the city for a bit. Go out to the Hamptons. But I told her the last thing I wanted to do was leave town. I didn't want to be alone. The attacks churned up old thoughts in my head." I nodded but said nothing in response. I felt we were encountering one another at a funeral; one never knows what to say to those who have been 10 bereaved. "I keep thinking about Chris," she went on. "I don't know why. Most nights I have to take something to help me rest. It's kind of like I've been thrown back a year." I suspect I looked alarmed because she smiled and added, "It's not *that* bad. I mean, I'm eating fine. I haven't lost it. But I feel haunted, you know?" 15

I considered her choice of words. "I have an aunt," I said, "my mother's most beautiful sister. Her marriage was arranged, so she had only met her husband a few times beforehand. He was an air force pilot. He died three months later, but she never married again. She said he was the love of her life." Erica appeared moved, both 20 touched and troubled by what I had said; leaning forward, she asked, "What's she like now?" "Mad," I said, "mad as a March hare." Erica stared; then she started to laugh – a surprised and delighted guffaw – and when she was done she placed her hand on mine. "I missed you," she said. "It's good to have you back." 25

I wanted to slip my fingers between hers, but I held my hand completely still, as though I was afraid any movement on my part might dislodge our connection. "Is she really mad?" Erica asked, raising an eyebrow and imitating my pronunciation of the word. "Yes, I am afraid," I said with mock solemnity, "utterly." This made 30 her smile; she suggested we order another bottle of wine. We

---

2 **confer sth. upon sb.**: *jdm. etwas verleihen*   8 **churn sth. up**: stir up
11 **bereaved**: having a close friend or relative who has died   22 **mad as a March hare** (infml): very crazy – hares (= *Hasen*) were called mad in March due to their strange behaviour during the mating season   28 **dislodge sth.**: break sth.
30 **mock** (adj): not sincere or real   **solemnity**: *Ernst*   **utterly**: totally, completely

lingered at our table until the restaurant closed for the night – by which time we were rather pleasantly drunk – and then strolled out into the street. "I love it when you talk about where you come from," she said, slipping her arm through mine, "you become so *alive*."
5 I did not say that the same could be said of her when she spoke of Chris; I did not say it because this fact elicited in me mixed emotions. On the one hand it pleased me as her friend to see her so animated, and I knew, moreover, that it was a mark of affection that she took me into her confidence in this way – I had never heard her discuss
10 Chris when speaking to someone else; on the other hand, I was desirous of embarking upon a relationship with her that amounted to more than friendship, and I felt in the strength of her ongoing attachment to Chris the presence of a rival – albeit a dead one – with whom I feared I could never compete. The aunt I had mentioned
15 was unlike Erica in almost every way: she was plump, insisted on traveling only by scooter, wore a backpack frequently crammed with goodies for her young nieces and nephews, and lived on a widow's small pension. But this was my aunt at forty-five; the woman who stared jauntily out of her photographs at the age of twenty-two was
20 cocksure and painfully attractive. I could only imagine how many suitors she had turned away, and I wondered if my infatuation with Erica was as doomed as theirs had been.

Erica's face was relaxed now; indeed she stifled a yawn as she leaned her head against my shoulder. But she had been tense at the
25 start of the evening, careworn and riddled with worry. Like so many others in the city after the attacks, she appeared deeply anxious. Yet her anxieties seemed only indirectly related to the prospect of dying at the hands of terrorists. The destruction of the World Trade Center

---

7 **animated** (adj): lively, full of energy   11 **embark upon sth.** (fml): start to do sth. new or difficult   13 **albeit** [ɑːlˈbiːɪt] (fml): although   15 **plump**: having a soft, round body; slightly fat   17 **goody** (infml): something nice to eat   19 **jaunty** [ˈdʒɔːnti]: showing that you are feeling confident and pleased with yourself
20 **cocksure** (infml, old-fashioned): overly confident   21 **suitor** [ˈsuːtər] (old-fashioned): a man who wants to marry a particular woman   22 **doomed**: certain to fail   23 **stifle sth.** [ˈstaɪfəl]: suppress sth.   23 **yawn** [jɑːn]: *Gähnen*
25 **careworn**: looking tired because you have a lot of worries   **riddled with sth.**: be full of sth., esp. sth. bad or unpleasant

had, as she had said, churned up old thoughts that had settled in the manner of sediment to the bottom of a pond; now the waters of her mind were murky with what previously had been ignored. I did not know if the same was true of me.

We wandered in silence through the night, and as luck would 5 have it – no, I am being dishonest; luck had nothing to do with it – we found ourselves outside my building. "Can I come up?" she asked. "I want to see where you live." I could hear my heart beating as we mounted the stairs; my studio was a fourth-floor walkup so, as you can well imagine, there were a great many to climb. I was 10 somewhat apprehensive of what she might think of the place – it was, after all, a tiny fraction of the size of her own home – but I reassured myself that it possessed a certain *literary* charm. "It's perfect," she said, sitting down on the edge of my futon, which was at that moment still in its extended position for use as a bed. 15

She shut her eyes, leaned back on her elbows, and smiled drowsily, in the manner of a trusting little girl. My bladder was dangerously close to bursting, and before dashing off to the lavatory I informed her I would return immediately. By the time I emerged, she was fast asleep. "Erica?" I said. There was no answer. I did not 20 know what to do, and hesitated before eventually turning off the light. The blinds were up; the nighttime glow of Manhattan found its way inside, and I watched the gentle rise and fall of her chest as she breathed. Then I covered her with a sheet and tossed a pillow on the floor for myself. I was exhausted, and suffering from jet lag in 25 addition, but I had long to wait before dreams took me. I did not wake in the morning when, as I later learned, she kissed me on the forehead before leaving.

But observe! A flower-seller approaches. I will summon him to our table. You are not in the mood? Surely you cannot object to a 30 single strand of jasmine buds. Here, take them in your hand: are they not like balls of velvet in their texture? More like popcorn

---

3 **murky**: not clear; dark or dirty with mud   11 **apprehensive**: worried or frightened that sth. unpleasant may happen   17 **drowsy**: tired and almost asleep **bladder**: *Harnblase*   25 **jet lag**: the feeling of being tired and slightly confused after a long plane journey   32 **velvet**: *Samt*   **texture**: the way a surface, substance or piece of cloth feels when you touch it

shrimp, you say? Ah, you jest; for an instant I thought you were
being serious. Yet you have succeeded in reminding me of a delicacy
we entirely lack in Lahore, being so far from the sea. What I would
not give for a bucket of American popcorn shrimp – fried in batter
5   until a delicious golden-brown and served with a sachet of tomato
sauce! – but sadly, I will have to content myself with these flowers
instead: so rare in New York, so common here.

Where was I? Yes, I was telling you of Erica and my return to
New York. After she had slept at my flat, Erica took to inviting me
10   out with pleasing regularity. I accompanied her to fundraisers for the
victims of the World Trade Center, dinners at the houses – for they
were houses, brownstones preserved as islands of single-family
accommodation amidst Manhattan's sea of apartments – of her
friends, openings and private viewings for patrons of the arts.
15   I became, in effect, her official escort at the events of New York
society.

This role pleased me indeed. I was presumptuous enough to
think that this was how my life was *meant* to be, that it had in some
way been inevitable that I should end up rubbing shoulders with the
20   truly wealthy in such exalted settings. Erica vouched for my
worthiness; my way of carrying myself – I flattered myself to
believe – suggested the impeccability of my breeding; and, for those
who inquired further, my Princeton degree and Underwood Samson
business card were invariably sufficient to earn me a respectful nod
25   of approval.

Looking back now, I see there was a certain symmetry to the
situation: I felt I was entering in New York the very same social class
that my family was falling out of in Lahore. Perhaps this accounted
for a good part of the comfort and satisfaction I found in my new
30   environment. But an even greater part of my happiness in those days
was due to being in the regular company of Erica. I could, without

---

1 **jest** (fml, old-fashioned): joke   4 **batter**: *Panade*   5 **sachet** [sæˈʃeɪ]: a small,
closed plastic or paper package   10 **fundraiser**: a social event held in order to
collect money for a charity or an organization   20 **vouch for sb./sth.** (fml): (here)
say that you believe that sb. is good enough to be there   21 **flatter yourself**: choose
to believe sth. good about yourself and your abilities   22 **impeccability**: perfectness
breeding: background, upbringing   24–25 **nod of approval**: *ein billigendes Nicken*

exaggeration, watch her for hours. The pride of her stance, the
slender muscularity of her arms and shoulders, the failure of her
garments to cloak the memory of those naked breasts I had seen in
Greece: all these things filled me with desire.

And yet I was also filled with protectiveness. Often, as we stood 5
or sat in the midst of an impeccably turned-out crowd, I would
observe that she was utterly detached, lost in a world of her own.
Her eyes were turned inward, and remarks made by her companions
would register only indirectly on her face, like the shadows of clouds
gliding across the surface of a lake. She smiled when it was brought 10
to her attention that she seemed distant, and said she was, as usual,
spacing out. But I had come to suspect that hers were not merely the
lapses of the absent-minded; no, she was struggling against a current
that pulled her within herself, and her smile contained the fear that
she might slip into her own depths, where she would be trapped, 15
unable to breathe. I wished to serve as her anchor in these moments,
without being so vulgar as to make known to her that this was a role
I felt she needed someone to play. I discovered that the best way of
doing this was to come close to touching her – to rest my hand on a
table, say, as near as possible to hers without actually making 20
contact – and then to wait for her to become aware of my physical
presence, at which point she would shake her head as if waking
from a dream and bridge the gap between us with a small caress.

Perhaps it was this sense of protectiveness that prevented my
attempting to kiss Erica; equally likely, it was the shyness and awe 25
that accompany first love. In any case, several weeks passed before
one night, after a Burmese meal in the East Village, Erica held me
back as her friends hailed taxis and began to disperse. "I have
something to tell you," she said. "I want to celebrate." "Why?"
I asked. "Because," she said, pressing her fingertips together and 30

1 **stance**: the way in which sb. stands   6 **impeccable**: perfect (here: in looks and/or
dress)   7 **detached** (adj): not involved in what is going on   12 **space out**: (here)
let your mind be elsewhere   13 **lapse**: short period of a particular behaviour
current (n): the movement of water in the sea or a river   16 **anchor** ['æŋkər]:
(here) a person or thing that gives sb. a feeling of safety   25 **awe** [ɑ:]: *Ehrfurcht*
28 **hail a taxi**: signal to a taxi to make it stop   **disperse**: move apart and go away in
different directions

smiling broadly, "I got an agent!" Her initial blind submissions had
been unsuccessful, she explained, but she had recently sent her
manuscript to an agency that represented a family friend; a junior
agent there had just this afternoon agreed to take her on. He said
5 length had been his only concern – the novella form being, in his
words, a platypus of a beast – but upon reflection he thought he
could make a strong case to publishers. I congratulated her and said
I would most willingly accompany her on any adventure she chose
for the evening; she suggested we purchase a magnum of champagne
10 and proceed to my flat, which was just around the corner.

She said this as though it was the most natural thing in the world;
I smiled assent in – as best I could manage – the same easy manner.
But it was clear to both of us, I think it safe to say, that a certain
gravity had attached itself to our actions, and I for one was
15 uncharacteristically clumsy as I searched in my pocket, first in a
liquor store for change, and later on the steps in front of my building
for my keys. It was a nippy October day and Erica was dressed
warmly; indoors, she removed her sleeveless jacket and her cotton
sweater, shedding layers until she achieved her preferred attire of
20 T-shirt and jeans. Lacking a candle, I turned on my television and set
it to mute, thereby bathing the room in a dim, flickering light. We
drank from a pair of ornate silver cups that had been a graduation
present from one of my uncles; the effect was to make the champagne
taste metallic, but in a not unpleasant – and indeed rather exotic –
25 fashion.

"I got banged up at tae kwon do practice today," Erica said. "We
were sparring, and I was up against this woman who's really quick.
She nailed me right under the armpit. Here," she touched herself,
"I can feel it when I breathe. It's a pretty good bruise." She looked at
30 me. I fingered my knee, following the scar left by my surgery. Then

---

6 **platypus of a beast**: *(hier) weder Fisch noch Fleisch* (**platypus**: *Schnabeltier*)
12 **assent**: agreement, approval   14 **gravity** (fml): seriousness   **attach yourself to
sth.**: connect yourself to sth.   15 **clumsy**: moving or doing things in a very
awkward way   17 **nippy**: cold   19 **shed sth.**: let sth. fall, get rid of sth.
21 **mute**: silent mode, with the sound off   22 **ornate**: covered with a lot of
decoration   26 **banged up** (adj): injured, hurt   27 **spar** (v): practice   28 **nail sb.**
(infml): hit sb.   29 **bruise** (n): *Prellung*

Erica said, "Do you want to see it?" I watched her, trying to determine whether she was joking; she did not seem to be. So I nodded, at that moment unable to trust my voice. I had thought she would merely raise her T-shirt; instead she pulled it off entirely and lifted one arm. I stared at her. I had seen her in a bikini before – indeed, I had seen 5 her topless – but as she sat on my futon in her bra I felt I had never seen her so naked. Her body had lost its tan and appeared almost blue in the glow of the television, and she was even more fit than I had remembered. She seemed otherworldly; she could have sprung from the pages of a graphic novel. I commanded myself to focus on 10 her bruise; it was dark and angry at the top of her rib cage, bisected by the strap of her bra.

Without thinking, I extended my hand. Then I hesitated. She returned my gaze watchfully, but her expression did not change, so I touched her, placing my fingers on her bruise. She rested her hand 15 on the back of her head as I traced the line of her ribs. I felt her skin break out in goose bumps, and I pulled her to me, embracing her gently and giving first her forehead, and then her lips, a kiss. She did not respond; she did not resist; she merely acceded as I undressed her. At times I would feel her hold on to me, or I would hear from 20 her the faintest of gasps. Mainly she was silent and unmoving, but such was my desire that I overlooked the growing wound this inflicted on my pride and continued. I found it difficult to enter her; it was as though she was not aroused. She said nothing while I was inside her, but I could see her discomfort, and so I forced myself to 25 stop.

"I'm sorry," she said. "No, I am sorry," I said. "You do not like it?" "I don't know," she said, and for the first time in my presence, her eyes filled with tears. "I just can't get wet. I don't know what's wrong with me." I held her in my arms, and as we lay there, she told me I 30 was the first man she had been with since Chris – indeed, *other* than

6 **bra**: *BH*   9 **otherworldly** (adj): *jenseitig*   10 **graphic novel**: novel in the form of a comic strip   11 **bisect sth.** ['baɪsekt]: divide sth. into two equal parts
19 **accede to sth.** (fml): agree to sth. (e.g. a request, proposal)   24 **aroused**: sexually excited   25 **discomfort**: unease

Chris. Her sexuality, she said, had been mostly dormant since his death. She had only once achieved orgasm, and that, too, by fantasizing of him. I did not know what to say. I wanted to console her, to accompany her into her mind and allow her to be less alone.
5   So I asked her to tell me about him, how they had come to kiss, how they had come to make love. "You really want to know?" she asked. I replied that I did, and so she told me.

I knew bits and pieces of their story from before; that night I received it whole. Something of it seemed familiar to me; later I
10   would realize what seemed familiar was the *emotion* with which she spoke, an emotion similar to that which she evoked in me. I attempted to separate myself from the situation, to listen to her as though I were not both aching for her and hurt that – seemingly despite herself – her body had rejected me. I succeeded in this to an
15   extent that surprises me still, when I think of it today. Their story remains vivid in my mind, but I will not recount it now. Suffice it to say that theirs had been an unusual love, with such a degree of commingling of identities that when Chris died, Erica felt she had lost herself; even now, she said, she did not know if she could be
20   found.

But as she spoke of him, her voice seemed to strengthen, and I felt her naked body soften and relax beside me. A liveliness entered her eyes; they ceased to be turned inward. She asked me about *my* experiences, about the nature of sex and relationships for teenagers
25   in Pakistan. I told her I had had next to nothing in the way of sex before coming to America, and my relationships hardly amounted to much in the face of what she had just recounted. But they were delightful in their own way, I said, and I entertained her with anecdotes of Lahore for what seemed like hours. At one point I
30   found myself gazing up at the ceiling as though I were gazing at the stars, and the two of us started to laugh. I felt we were at last becoming comfortable in the same bed, and as the sky outside began

1 **dormant**: asleep, inactive   3 **console sb.**: give comfort or sympathy to sb. who is unhappy or disappointed   14 **reject sb.**: refuse sb. as a lover   18 **commingling** (adj): mixing

to lighten, I was compelled to stifle a good-natured yawn. She, too, was drowsy, she said, adding that I was better than any medication at putting her at ease. We fell asleep like that, not in one another's arms, but shoulder to shoulder, with our knuckles touching at our sides. Perhaps because of our conversation I dreamed not of Erica, 5 but of home; what she dreamed of I did not know …

But I observe, sir, that you are watching me with a rather peculiar expression. Possibly you find me crass for revealing such intimacies to you, a stranger? No? I will interpret that movement of your head as a response in the negative. Allow me to assure you that I do not 10 always speak this openly; indeed, I almost never do. But tonight, as I think we both understand, is a night of some *importance*. Certainly I perceive it to be so – and yet if I am wrong, you will surely be justified in regarding me the most terrible boor!

---

1 **compel sb.**: force sb. to do sth.   2 **drowsy**: sleepy, tired and almost asleep
4 **knuckle**: the joints in the fingers   8 **crass**: insensitive   14 **boor** [bʊr] (old-fashioned): a rude unpleasant person

7

I wonder now, sir, whether I believed at all in the firmness of the foundations of the new life I was attempting to construct for myself in New York. Certainly I *wanted* to believe; at least I wanted not to disbelieve with such an intensity that I prevented myself as much as
5 was possible from making the obvious connection between the crumbling of the world around me and the impending destruction of my personal American dream. The power of my blinders shocks me, looking back – so stark in retrospect were the portents of coming disaster in the news, on the streets, and in the state of the woman
10 with whom I had become enamored.

America was gripped by a growing and self-righteous rage in those weeks of September and October as I cavorted about with Erica; the mighty host I had expected of your country was duly raised and dispatched – but homeward, towards my family in
15 Pakistan. When I spoke to them on the telephone, my mother was frightened, my brother was angry, and my father was stoical – this would all pass, he said. I found reassurance in my father's views, and I dressed myself in them as though they were my own. "Are you worried, man?" Wainwright asked me one day in the Underwood
20 Samson cafeteria, resting his hand on my shoulder in a gesture of concern as I filled a bagel with smoked salmon and cream cheese. No, I explained, Pakistan had pledged its support to the United States, the Taliban's threats of retaliation were meaningless, my family would be just fine.

6 **crumbling**: falling apart   **impending** (adj): that is going to happen very soon
7 **blinders** (AE, pl): pieces of leather that are placed at the side of a horse's eyes to stop it from looking sideways   8 **stark**: clear   **portent** ['pɔːrtent] (fml): omen, a sign or warning of sth. that is going to happen in the future   10 **enamored with sb.** [ɪnˈæmərd] (fml): in love with sb.   11 **self-righteous**: *selbstgerecht*   12 **cavort** [kəˈvɔːrt]: move around in a noisy, excited and often sexual way   13 **host**: a large number of things (here: an army)   16 **stoical**: *stoisch*   22 **pledge sth.**: formally promise to give or do sth.   23 **retaliation**: *Vergeltung*

I ignored as best I could the rumors I overheard at the Pak-Punjab Deli: Pakistani cabdrivers were being beaten to within an inch of their lives; the FBI was raiding mosques, shops, and even people's houses; Muslim men were disappearing, perhaps into shadowy detention centers for questioning or worse. I reasoned that these 5 stories were mostly untrue; the few with some basis in fact were almost certainly being exaggerated; and besides, those rare cases of abuse that regrettably did transpire were unlikely ever to affect me because such things invariably happened, in America as in all countries, to the hapless poor, not to Princeton graduates earning 10 eighty thousand dollars a year.

Thus clad in my armor of denial I was able to focus – with continuing and noteworthy success – on my job. After the exceptional review I received for my performance in the Philippines, I had become Jim's fair-haired boy. He offered me another assignment 15 on one of his teams, this time valuing an ailing cable operator. The firm was based in New Jersey – to which I began a daily commute – and had been hit hard by the decline in investor sentiment surrounding the technology sector in general and small-scale broadband providers in particular; it was barely able to service its 20 debts and had become a prime candidate for acquisition.

On this occasion, our client was unconcerned with the potential for future growth. No, our mandate was to determine how much fat could be cut. Call centers, it was evident, could be outsourced; truck rolls could be reduced; purchasing could be consolidated with our 25 client's existing operations. The potential for headcount reduction was substantial – and hence the reception our team received from the employees of the company was frosty indeed. Our telephone

---

5 **detention center**: place where people are kept for questioning   8 **transpire**: become known   10 **hapless**: not lucky, unfortunate   12 **armor**: special metal clothing for protection that soldiers wore in the past   **denial**: a refusal to accept that sth. unpleasant or painful is true   15 **fair-haired boy**: person who is the favourite of sb.   16 **ailing**: having problems and getting weaker   17 **commute** (n): the journey that a person makes when they go to work   21 **acquisition**: the act of buying a company   23 **mandate**: task   24–25 **truck roll**: act of having a technician come over to do some piece of work   25 **consolidate sth.**: *etwas zusammenlegen* 26 **headcount reduction**: *Personalabbau*

extensions and fax machines would mysteriously stop working; our security badges and notebooks would disappear. Often I would emerge into the car park to find that one of the tires of my rental car was punctured – far too often for it to be mere coincidence.

5   Once this happened when Jim had come out for the day; he had asked me to give him a ride back to the city. He shook his head as I brought out the spare. "Don't let it get you down, Changez," he said. "Time only moves in one direction. Remember that. Things always change." He loosened the metal strap of his watch, a solid, diver's
10   chronometer, and let it slide to his knuckles. "When I was in college," he went on, "the economy was in bad shape. It was the seventies. Stagflation. But you could just smell the opportunity. America was shifting from manufacturing to services, a huge shift, bigger than anything we'd ever seen. My father had lived and died making things
15   with his hands, so I knew from up close that that time was past." He refastened the clasp of his watch. Then he made a fist and twisted his thick forearm from side to side, slowly, until the instrument found its level. There was an almost ritualistic quality to his movements, like a batsman – or even, I would say, a knight – donning his gloves
20   before striding onto a field of contest.

"The economy's an animal," Jim continued. "It evolves. First it needed muscle. Now all the blood it could spare was rushing to its brain. That's where I wanted to be. In finance. In the coordination business. And that's where *you* are. You're blood brought from some
25   part of the body that the species doesn't need anymore. The tailbone. Like me. We came from places that were wasting away." I had finished replacing the tire, so I shut the boot and unlocked the doors. "Most people don't recognize that, kid," he said, buckling himself in beside me and nodding his head in the direction of the
30   darkened building we had left. "They try to resist change. Power comes from *becoming* change."

---

7 **spare**: an extra tire that you keep in case you need to replace one   12 **stagflation**: an economic situation where there is high inflation (= prices rising continuously) but no increase in the jobs that are available or in business activity   16 **clasp**: a device that fastens sth.   19 **batsman**: (in sport) the player who has to hit the ball   **don sth.** (fml): put on sth (esp. clothes)   20 **contest**: competition   25 **tailbone**: *Rückgrat*   28–29 **buckle yourself in**: fasten your seat belt

I considered what Jim had said – both that evening, on the drive to Manhattan, and in the weeks that followed. There was a certain ring of truth to his words, but I was uncomfortable with the idea that the place I came from was condemned to atrophy. So I dwelled instead on the positive aspect of his little sermon: on the idea that I 5 had chosen a field of endeavor that would be of ever-greater importance to humanity and would be likely, therefore, to provide me with ever-increasing returns. I also found myself better equipped to regard as misguided – or at least myopic – the resentment which seethed around us as we went about our business that autumn in 10 that New Jersey corporate park.

But it would not be true to say I was completely untroubled. There were older people among the workers of the cable company. I sometimes sat near them in the cafeteria – although never at the same table; the seats beside our team always went untaken – and I 15 imagined many of them had children my age. If English had a respectful form of the word *you* – as we do in Urdu – I would have used it to address them without the slightest hesitation. As it was, the nature of our interactions left me with minimal scope to show them deference – or even sympathy. I remarked upon this to 20 Wainwright on one of the many weekend nights we found ourselves spending at the office, and he said, "You're working for the *man*, buddy. Didn't anyone tell you that at orientation?" Then he gave me a tired smile and added, "But I get where you're coming from. Just remember your deals would go ahead whether you worked on them 25 or not. And focus on the fundamentals."

Focus on the fundamentals. This was Underwood Samson's guiding principle, drilled into us since our first day at work. It mandated a

---

4 **be condemned to sth.**: be forced into sth. (e.g. a difficult or unpleasant situation) **atrophy**: *Schwund, Verkümmerung*   5 **sermon**: moral advice given by a person in a long talk   8 **return**: profit   9 **myopic** [maɪˈɑːpɪk]: short-sighted   **resentment**: feeling of anger or unhappiness about sth. that you think is unfair   10 **seethe** (fml): *brodeln*   18 **hesitation**: slow reaction to sth. due to a feeling of uncertainty
19 **scope**: *(Handlungs-)Spielraum*   20 **deference**: behaviour that shows that you respect sb./sth.   26 **fundamentals** (pl): a basic rule or principle; an essential part
28 **mandate sth.**: give an order that sth. must be done

single-minded attention to financial detail, teasing out the true
nature of those drivers that determine an asset's value. And that was
precisely what I continued to do, more often than not with both skill
and enthusiasm. Because to be perfectly honest, sir, the
5 compassionate pangs I felt for soon-to-be-redundant workers were
not overwhelming in their frequency; our job required a degree of
commitment that left one with rather limited time for such
distractions.

But then, in the latter part of October, something happened that
10 upset my equanimity. It was shortly after Erica and I had abortively
attempted to make love – perhaps a day or two later, although I can
no longer precisely recall. The bombing of Afghanistan had already
been under way for a fortnight, and I had been avoiding the evening
news, preferring not to watch the partisan and sports-event-like
15 coverage given to the mismatch between the American bombers
with their twenty-first-century weaponry and the ill-equipped and
ill-fed Afghan tribesmen below. On those rare occasions when I did
find myself confronted by such programming – in a bar, say, or at the
entrance to the cable company's offices – I was reminded of the film
20 *Terminator,* but with the roles reversed so that the machines were
cast as heroes.

What left me shaken, however, occurred when I turned on the
television myself. I had reached home from New Jersey after
midnight and was flipping through the channels, looking for a
25 soothing sitcom, when I chanced upon a newscast with ghostly
night-vision images of American troops dropping into Afghanistan

---

1 **single-minded**: only thinking about one particular aim or goal because you are
determined to achieve sth.   **tease sth. out**: *etwas herauskitzeln/hervorlocken*
2 **driver**: decisive factor   5 **compassionate**: feeling or showing sympathy for people
who are suffering   **pang**: a sudden strong feeling of physical or emotional pain
7 **commitment**: the willingness to work hard and give your energy and time to a job
or an activity   10 **equanimity** [ˌekwəˈnɪmətɪ] (fml): calm state of mind so you do
not become angry or upset   **abortively** (fml): unsuccessfully   13 **fortnight**: two
weeks   14 **partisan** [ˈpɑːrtəzən] (adj): one-sided   15 **mismatch**: *Ungleichgewicht,
Missverhältnis*   16 **ill-equipped** (adj): not having the necessary equipment
20 **reverse sth.**: turn sth. the opposite way around   21 **cast sb.**: choose sb. as an
actor in a film

for what was described as a daring raid on a Taliban command post.
My reaction caught me by surprise; Afghanistan was Pakistan's
neighbor, our friend, and a fellow Muslim nation besides, and the
sight of what I took to be the beginning of its invasion by your
countrymen caused me to tremble with fury. I had to sit down to   5
calm myself, and I remember polishing off a third of a bottle of
whiskey before I was able to fall asleep.

The next morning I was, for the first time, late for work. I had
overslept and woken with a cracking headache. My fury had ebbed,
but much though I wished to pretend I had imagined it entirely, I   10
was no longer capable of so thorough a self-deception. I did,
however, tell myself that I had overreacted, that there was nothing I
could do, and that all these world events were playing out on a stage
of no relevance to my personal life. But I remained aware of the
embers glowing within me, and that day I found it difficult to   15
concentrate on the pursuit – at which I was normally so capable – of
fundamentals.

But listen! Did you hear that, sir, a muffled growl, as if of a young
lion held captive in a gunnysack? That was my stomach protesting at
going unfed. Let us now order our dinner. You would rather wait,   20
you say, and eat upon your return to your hotel? But I insist! You
must not pass up such an authentic introduction to Lahori cuisine; it
will, given the dishes for which this market is justifiably renowned,
be a purely carnivorous feast – one that harks back to an era before
man's knowledge of cholesterol made him fearful of his prey – and   25
all the more delectable for it.

Perhaps because we currently lack wealth, power, or even
sporting glory – the occasional brilliance of our temperamental
cricket team notwithstanding – commensurate with our status as the
world's sixth most populous country, we Pakistanis tend to take an   30

---

1 **daring** (adj): brave, courageous   **raid**: a short surprise attack   9 **ebb**: decrease
15 **embers** (pl): *Glut*   16 **pursuit**: the act of looking for or trying to find sth.
19 **gunnysack**: a large bag made from rough material and used to store flour,
potatoes, etc.   24 **carnivorous** [kɑːrˈnɪvərəs]: feeding on meat   **hark back to sth.**:
be like sth. in the past   26 **delectable**: delicious   29 **commensurate with sth.**
[kəˈmensərət] (fml): matching sth. in size, importance, quality, etc.

inordinate pride in our food. Here in Old Anarkali that pride is visible in the purity of the fare on offer; not one of these worthy restaurateurs would consider placing a western dish on his menu. No, we are surrounded instead by the kebab of mutton, the tikka of
5 chicken, the stewed foot of goat, the spiced brain of sheep! These, sir, are *predatory* delicacies, delicacies imbued with a hint of luxury, of wanton abandon. Not for us the vegetarian recipes one finds across the border to the east, nor the sanitized, sterilized, processed meats so common in your homeland! Here we are not squeamish
10 when it comes to facing the consequences of our desire.

For we were not always burdened by debt, dependent on foreign aid and handouts; in the stories we tell of ourselves we were not the crazed and destitute radicals you see on your television channels but rather saints and poets and – yes – conquering kings. *We* built the
15 Royal Mosque and the Shalimar Gardens in this city, and *we* built the Lahore Fort with its mighty walls and wide ramp for our battle-elephants. And we did these things when your country was still a collection of thirteen small colonies, gnawing away at the edge of a continent.

20 But once more I am raising my voice, and making you rather uncomfortable besides. I apologize; it was not my intention to be rude. In any case, I ought instead to be explaining to you why I did not speak to Erica of my fury at seeing American troops enter Afghanistan. After that night when we celebrated in my bed her

2 **fare** (old-fashioned): food that is offered as a meal   4 **mutton**: meat from a fully grown sheep   **tikka**: type of spicy Asian marinade   5 **stewed**: *geschmort, gedünstet*   6 **predatory** ['predətəri]: living by killing and eating other animals **imbue sb./sth. with sth.** [ɪm'bjuː]: fill sb./sth. with sth. (e.g. strong feelings, opinions or values)   7 **wanton** (old-fashioned): behaving in a very immoral way **abandon** (n, fml): *Hingabe*   8 **sanitized** (adj): thoroughly cleaned   8–9 **processed meat**: meat which has been preserved for mass consumption   9 **squeamish**: easily upset or made to feel sick by unpleasant sights or situations   11 **burdened with sth.**: carrying sth. heavy   12 **handout**: food, money or clothes that are given to a person who is poor   13 **crazed** (fml): full of strong feelings and lacking control **destitute**: without money, food and the other things necessary for life   15 **Royal Mosque**: one of the world's largest mosques built in 1673   **Shalimar Gardens**: a Persian garden built in 1641   16 **Lahore Fort**: a citadel in the Walled City of Lahore   18 **gnaw away at sth.**: keep eating sth. bit by bit

obtaining an agent, I had no contact with Erica for several days; she
did not answer when I rang and she did not respond to my messages.
I was hurt by this behavior – taking her silence for inconsideration –
and I arrived in a reproachful mood for the drink that she eventually
did invite me to. I was utterly unprepared for what I saw.   5

At the counter was a diminished Erica, not the vivid, confident
woman I knew but a pale, nervous creature who could almost have
been a stranger. She seemed to have lost weight and her eyes darted
about the bar. It was not until she smiled that something of the old
Erica glimmered within her, but her smile left her face as quickly as   10
it had come. My consternation must have been evident because she
smiled again and said, "Do I look that bad?" "Not at all," I lied, "just
tired, perhaps. Have you been unwell?" "Yeah," she said. "I'm sorry I
didn't get back to you sooner." "That is quite all right," I said. "I hope
I was not a pest." "Never," she said. "I've been going through a bad   15
patch. It's happened before. But it hasn't been like this since the first
time, after Chris died."

We ordered, beer for myself and a bottle of water for her, and I
considered giving her an embrace but decided against it; she seemed
too brittle to be touched. "What happens is," she went on, "my mind   20
starts to go in circles, thinking and thinking, and then I can't sleep.
And once a couple of days go by, if you haven't slept, you start to get
sick. You can't eat. You start to cry. It just feeds on itself. I've got
some stronger stuff from the doctor, so I've been sleeping again. But
it isn't real sleep. And the rest of the day I feel like I'm out of it. Like   25
when you get off a plane and you can't hear properly. Like that,
except it's not just my hearing, and I can't pop my ears." She took a
sip of her water and managed to wink at me. Then she said, "Freaky,
huh?"

I stood there in silence, unable to think of what to say or even to   30
offer her a smile; I was horrified. But she was waiting for me to

---

1 **obtain sth.**: get sth.   3 **inconsideration**: *Rücksichtslosigkeit*   4 **reproachful**:
expressing blame or criticism   **mood**: the way you are feeling at a particular time
6 **diminished**: shrunken, appearing smaller   11 **consternation** (fml): a worried
feeling after you have received an unpleasant surprise   15–16 **bad patch** (infml): a
difficult or unhappy period of time   19 **embrace** (n): *Umarmung*   20 **brittle**: hard
but easily broken   28 **wink**: *zwinkern*

respond, so I said, "But what is it you think of that causes you to become so upset?" "I think of Chris a lot," she said, "and I think of me. I think of my book. I think some pretty dark thoughts, sometimes. And I think of you." "What do you think of," I asked,
5   "when you think of me?" "I think it isn't good for you to see me so much right now," she answered. "I mean it isn't good for you." "No," I reassured her, although I was frightened, "I want to see you." "That's what I mean," she said, looking into my eyes with great seriousness. "Do you get it? That's what I mean."

10   I did not get it in the least, and I asked her to come home with me. "I don't think I should," she said. "Really." But there was a softness in her expression, and when I continued to insist, she finally did acquiesce. During our taxi ride my mind struggled to comprehend what was happening. I had over these past weeks –
15   sentimental and old-fashioned as it may sound, but then I was raised in a family where brief courtships were the norm – been indulging in daydreams of a life as Erica's husband; now I found not just those daydreams but the woman herself vanishing before my eyes. I wanted to help her, to hold on to her – indeed, I wanted to hold on
20   to us – and I was desperate to extricate her from the maze of her psychosis. But I did not know how to proceed.

In my bed she asked me to put my arms around her, and I did so, speaking quietly in her ear. I knew she enjoyed my stories of Pakistan, so I rambled on about my family and Lahore. When I tried
25   to kiss her, she did not move her lips or shut her eyes. So I shut them for her and asked, "Are you missing Chris?" She nodded, and I saw tears begin to force themselves between her lashes. "Then pretend," I said, "pretend I am him." I do not know why I said it; I felt overcome and it seemed, suddenly, a possible way forward.
30   "What?" she said, but she did not open her eyes. "Pretend I am him," I said again. And slowly, in darkness and in silence, we did.

---

13 **acquiesce** [ˌækwi'es] (fml): accept sth. without arguing   16 **courtship** (old-fashioned): the time when two people have a romantic relationship before they get married   20 **extricate sb. from sth.**: free sb./sth. from sth. which makes them feel trapped   21 **psychosis** [saɪ'koʊsɪs]: mental illness   28 **pretend**: behave as if sth. that is not true is true   29 **overcome**: *überwältigt*

I do not know how to describe my experience of what happened next; I cannot, of course, claim that I was *possessed*, but at the same time I did not seem to be myself. It was as though we were under a spell, transported to a world where I was Chris and she was with Chris, and we made love with a physical intimacy that Erica and I 5 had never enjoyed. Her body denied mine no longer; I watched her shut eyes, and her shut eyes watched *him*.

I can still recall her muscularity, made more pronounced by her gauntness, and the near-inanimate smoothness and coolness of her flesh as she leaned back and exposed to my touch her breasts. The 10 entrance between her legs was wet and dilated, but was at the same time oddly rigid; it reminded me – unwillingly – of a wound, giving our sex a violent undertone despite the gentleness with which I attempted to move. More than once I smelled what I thought to be blood, but when I reached down to ascertain with my fingers 15 whether it was her time of month, I found them unstained. She shuddered towards the end – grievously, almost mortally; her shuddering called forth my own.

"You're a kind person," she said afterwards, as we lay there. "It sounds like a stupid thing to say but it's true." I held her and did not 20 reply. I felt something I have not felt before or since; I remember it well: I felt at once both *satiated* and *ashamed*. My satiation was understandable to me; my shame was more confusing. Perhaps, by taking on the persona of another, I had diminished myself in my own eyes; perhaps I was humiliated by the continuing dominance, 25 in the strange romantic triangle of which I found myself a part, of my dead rival; perhaps I was worried that I had acted selfishly and I sensed, even then, that I had done Erica some terrible harm. But this

---

2 **possessed**: controlled by a spirit   3–4 **under a spell**: affected by magic
9 **gauntness**: state of being very thin, usu. because of illness, hunger or worry
near-inanimate [ɪn'ænɪmət]: almost dead or appearing to be dead   15 **ascertain sth.** (fml): find out true or correct information about sth.   16 **unstained**: clean
17 **grievously** (adv, fml): very serious and often causing great pain or suffering
mortally: indicating the arrival of death   22 **satiated** ['seɪʃieɪtɪd] (adj): having had so much of sth. that you do not feel you want any more   25 **humiliate sb.**: make sb. feel ashamed or stupid and lose the respect of other people

last explanation is – I hope – unlikely; surely I could not have known what would happen to her over the weeks and months to follow.

Erica fell asleep that night without medication; I remained awake, in part because I had not yet eaten. I hesitated to rise and go to the
5 refrigerator for fear of disturbing her, but her sleep was deep, like that of a child, and eventually I managed. I ate only bread and drank only water, a tasteless meal, but I kept at it until my belly was full, and when I returned to the bed it was as though I had a tight drum strapped to my front, which forced me to lie on my side.

10 It is impossible to tell, sir, given the gloom about us and the unexpressive cast of your face, but I suspect you are looking at me with a degree of revulsion; certainly I would look at you in such a manner if *you* had just told me what I have told you. But I hope your disgust has not banished your appetite, for I am summoning our
15 waiter to take our order. Tonight, I can assure you, our meal will be anything but tasteless – and here he comes. Good man!

---

11 **cast**: *Abdruck* 12 **revulsion**: a strong feeling of disgust or horror 14 **banish sb./sth.**: force sb./sth. to go away

8

I observe, sir, that there continues to be something about our waiter that puts you ill at ease. I will admit that he is an intimidating chap, larger even than you are. But the hardness of his weathered face can readily be accounted for: he hails from our mountainous northwest, where life is far from easy. And if you should sense that he has taken 5 a disliking to you, I would ask you to be so kind as to ignore it; his tribe merely spans both sides of our border with neighboring Afghanistan, and has suffered during offensives conducted by your countrymen.

Is he praying, you ask? No, sir, not at all! His recitation – 10 rhythmic, formulaic, from memory, and so, I will concede, not unlike a prayer – is in actuality an attempt to transmit orally our menu, much as in your country one is told the specials. Here, of course, there are no specials; the excellent establishment of which tonight we are patrons has in all likelihood prepared precisely the 15 same dishes for many years. I could translate for you but perhaps it would be better if I selected a number of delicacies for us to share. You will grant me that honor? Thank you. There, it is done, and off he goes.

I had been telling you of my disquiet on the night I finally made 20 love to Erica – a night that ought, were ours a more normal relationship, to have been one of great joy. She left before dawn, waking with a start and insisting that she return home despite my requests that she stay. Once again, considerable time would pass before I heard from her again; my calls went unanswered, my 25 messages unreturned. I had learned my lesson, and I desisted from

---

4 **hail from** (fml): come from or have been born in a particular place   11 **concede**: admit that sth. is true, logical, etc   18 **grant sth.**: agree to give sb. what they ask for   20 **disquiet** (fml): feelings of worry and unhappiness about sth.   26 **desist from sth.** (fml): stop doing sth.

attempting to make contact. But once a fortnight had gone by, I tried again and was rewarded by a response. She apologized, as she had previously done, for disappearing in this fashion; she said she thought it best, perhaps for her but certainly also for me, that we try
5 not to see each other too often; and she consented to my request that we meet. "But come over to my place," she said. "I don't feel up to going out."

I was greeted at the door to Erica's apartment by her mother, who ushered me into an antechamber – which featured, among its
10 antique decorations, a bonsai tree and a harpsichord – and said, "I think we need to chat. Erica has told you about her history, yes?" I nodded. "Well," she went on, "her condition has come back. It's serious. What she needs right now is stability. No emotional upheavals, you get me? I can see you're a nice young man. And I
15 know she cares about you. But you have to understand that she's a sick girl at the moment. She doesn't need a boyfriend. She needs a friend." She looked at me beseechingly. "I understand, madam," I said. "I will do whatever you think best for her." "Thank you," she said. Then she smiled and added, "It's easy to tell why she likes you."

20 That conversation had a considerable impact on me, not so much for what was said – although I was alarmed by this grave characterization of Erica's situation – but for *how* it was said; Erica's mother's tone was one of quiet desperation, and it frightened me. I entered Erica's room tentatively, attempting to steel myself against
25 what I might find. What I found was not at first particularly alarming: Erica reclined on her bed, pale, yes, as though she had a fever, and with hair that had gone some time since it was last washed, but seemingly in good spirits. She patted the space beside her and offered me her forehead to kiss as I sat down.

30 We spoke for a while as though nothing unusual had happened and we were meeting under the most ordinary of circumstances. I told her about my project in New Jersey – the negative reaction to

9 **antechamber** [ˈænti̩tʃeɪmbər]: a room where people can wait before entering a larger room   14 **upheaval**: a big change that causes a lot of confusion and worry
17 **beseeching** [biˈsiːtʃɪŋ] (fml): *flehentlich*   24 **tentative**: hesitant   **steel yourself for sth.**: prepare yourself for sth. unpleasant   26 **recline** (fml): sit or lie in a relaxed way, with your body leaning backwards

our presence by the employees of the cable company, Jim's words of
advice – and about the day-to-day occurrences in my life since she
had seen me last. She told me about her doctor and her medication,
how the drugs made it difficult to concentrate and so her days
seemed to slip away with nothing to show for them. Given the   5
relaxed manner in which she described it an observer would have
been forgiven for thinking that her condition was not serious and
she was on the mend – until I asked about her novel.

I immediately regretted doing so. Her eyes began to wander, and
her voice became less sure. "I can't seem to work on it," she said.   10
"Every time I try, I just get upset. I haven't been taking my agent's
calls. Poor guy. He must think I'm a lunatic." I remarked that writers
were known to be eccentric and so it was unlikely her agent was
particularly perturbed, and then I tried to change the subject, but
she would not have it. "It doesn't help anymore," she said. "I used to   15
turn to it, my writing, when I needed to get something out that was
stuck inside. But I can't get it out now. It pulls me in, you know?
I dwell on it instead of writing it." I tried to prevent myself from
asking her what *it* was – whether because I thought it would upset
her or because I thought it would upset me, I do not now know –   20
but I failed. "It's whether there's something left," she explained,
suddenly and unsettlingly calm, "or whether it's all already
happened."

How can I describe to you, sir, how much her words disturbed
me? She glanced away, and I saw her recede into her mind. I placed   25
my hand next to hers, hoping as I had done innumerable times in
the past to lure her out of her thoughts. I watched our skin – mine
healthy and brown, hers sickly white – separated by a distance not
greater than the width of an engagement ring, but she did not notice
me. I waited for my proximity to make itself felt to her; a minute   30
passed in this fashion. Then she removed her hand from where it lay

---

2 **occurrence**: *Geschehnis, Begebenheit*   5 **with nothing to show for**: with no real
successful results   8 **on the mend** (infml): getting better after an illness or injury
14 **perturb sb.** [pər'tɜ:b] (fml): make sb. worried or anxious   25 **recede** [ri:'si:d]:
move gradually away   27 **lure sb.** [lʊər]: persuade or trick sb. to go somewhere or
to do sth. by promising them a reward

and – without ever looking in my direction – covered it with her other hand on her lap.

When Erica's mother entered shortly thereafter, I did not feel she was interrupting. No, she was not preventing the continuation of a
5 discussion between her daughter and myself; she was merely bringing to an end my intrusion on a conversation Erica was having with Chris – a conversation occurring on some plane that I could not reach or even properly see. Erica waved a good-bye to me as I left her room, but she did so with her face averted, so I could not
10 meet her gaze. Her mother thanked me for coming and asked me to wait for Erica to contact me before coming again. And with that, and a gentle kiss on the cheek, the door to the elevator was shut upon me and I began to travel down the shaft, alone.

I returned to my apartment and spent that night in semidarkness,
15 in the glow of the city's lights entering through my windows, wondering as I would wonder for many months thereafter – indeed, as I sometimes wonder to this day – where Erica was going. I never came to know what triggered her decline – was it the trauma of the attack on her city? the act of sending out her book in search of
20 publication? the echoes raised in her by our lovemaking? all of these things? none of them? – but I think I knew even then that she was disappearing into a powerful *nostalgia,* one from which only she could choose whether or not to return.

For it was clear Erica needed something that I – even by
25 consenting to play the part of a man not myself – was unable to give her. In all likelihood she longed for her adolescence with Chris, for a time before his cancer made her aware of impermanence and mortality. Perhaps the reality of their time together was as wonderful as she had, on more than one occasion, described to me. Or perhaps
30 theirs was a past all the more potent for its being imaginary. I did not know whether I believed in the truth of their love; it was, after all, a religion that would not accept me as a convert. But I knew that *she*

---

6 **intrusion**: the act of entering a place which is private or where you may not be wanted   18 **trigger sth.**: cause sth. to happen suddenly   27 **impermanence**: quality of not lasting or stay the same forever   32 **convert**: a person who has changed his or her religion

believed in it, and I felt small for being able to offer her nothing of comparable splendor instead.

I did not see Erica again that year. Thanksgiving soon gave way to the chill of December, and every week – every day – I thought of calling her but prevented myself from doing so. Her mother had, of course, asked me to resist, and I suspect I thought, given the catastrophic progress of our relationship thus far, that imposing myself on her interior struggle would only do her harm. But I must admit that my motives were not entirely noble; there were in me at least some elements of the anger and hurt vanity that characterize a spurned lover, and these unworthy sentiments helped me to keep my distance. Still, I remained concerned for Erica's well-being – and remained also in the grip of a certain, probably irrational, *hope* – so the ongoing task of abstaining from communication was a struggle not unlike that of a man attempting to rid himself of an addiction.

Possibly this was due to my state of mind, but it seemed to me that America, too, was increasingly giving itself over to a dangerous nostalgia at that time. There was something undeniably retro about the flags and uniforms, about generals addressing cameras in war rooms and newspaper headlines featuring such words as *duty* and *honor*. I had always thought of America as a nation that looked forward; for the first time I was struck by its determination to look *back*. Living in New York was suddenly like living in a film about the Second World War; I, a foreigner, found myself staring out at a set that ought to be viewed not in Technicolor but in grainy black and white. What your fellow countrymen longed for was unclear to me – a time of unquestioned dominance? of safety? of moral certainty? I did not know – but that they were scrambling to don the costumes of another era was apparent. I felt treacherous for wondering whether

---

2 **splendor**: grand and impressive beauty   7-8 **impose yourself on sb.**: force yourself into the company of sb.   10 **vanity**: too much pride in your own appearance, abilities or achievements   11 **spurned**: rejected, turned down   14 **abstain from sth.**: decide not to do sth., esp. sth. you like   18 **undeniable**: true, certain   **retro**: using styles or fashions from the recent past   25 **Technicolor**: *Farbe*   **grainy**: *körnig*   28 **scramble**: move quickly but with difficulty to do sth.   29 **treacherous** ['tretʃərəs]: *verräterisch*

that era was fictitious, and whether – if it could indeed be animated – it contained a part written for someone like me.

But what is that? Ah, your unusual telephone, beeping a demand for your attention. No, sir, I do not mind in the least; please proceed
5　to key in your reply. It occurs to me that you have been contacted with the precision of an old church bell tower, by which I mean precisely on the hour – perhaps the company is checking up on you? No, you need not answer. But now that your response has been sent, allow me to direct your gaze to that grill where at this very moment
10　our boneless chicken pieces are being set to roast. Observe the sparks that fly from the coals, angry and red, as our cook fans the flames. It is quite a beautiful sight, you must admit, and with it will soon come – *there*, do you smell it? – the most mouth-watering of aromas.

15　I had been telling you of the nostalgia that was becoming so prevalent in my world at the onset of the final winter I would spend in your country. But one notable bulwark continued to hold firm against this sentiment: Underwood Samson, which occupied most of my waking hours, and which was – as an institution – not nostalgic
20　whatsoever. At work we went about the task of shaping the future with little regard for the past, and my personal efficacy continued to grow as I immersed myself in my project at the cable company, hoping, in this way, to leave behind the many worries that preyed upon me when I was free to ruminate.

25　I suspect I was never better at the pursuit of fundamentals than I was at that time, analyzing data as though my life depended on it. Our creed was one which valued above all else maximum productivity, and such a creed was for me doubly reassuring because

---

1 **era** ['ɪrə]: a period of time, usu. in history, that is different from other periods because of particular characteristics or events　5 **key in sth.**: enter sth. on a computer or mobile phone　16 **onset**: the beginning of sth.　17 **bulwark** ['bʊlwərk] (fml): a person or thing that protects or defends sth.　17–18 **hold firm against sth.**: *gegen etwas standhalten*　18 **sentiment**: a feeling or an opinion, esp. one that is based on emotions　21 **efficacy** ['efɪkəsi]: effectiveness　23–24 **prey on sb.'s mind**: make sb. think and worry about sth. all the time　24 **ruminate** (fml): think deeply about things　27 **creed**: a set of principles or religious beliefs

it was quantifiable – and hence *knowable* – in a period of great
uncertainty, and because it remained utterly convinced of the
possibility of progress while others longed for a sort of *classical*
period that had come and gone, if it had ever existed at all. I detected
a change in my attitude to my colleagues, a greater understanding of   5
what drove them to focus so completely on their professional lives,
and perhaps as a consequence it seemed for a while that my
popularity at the office was on the rise.

    Yet even at Underwood Samson I could not entirely escape the
growing importance of *tribe*. Once I was walking to my rental car in   10
the parking lot of the cable company when I was approached by a
man I did not know. He made a series of unintelligible noises –
"*akhala-malakhala*," perhaps, or "*khalapal-khalapala*" – and pressed
his face alarmingly close to mine. I shifted my stance, presenting
him with my side and raising my hands to shoulder height; I thought   15
he might be mad, or drunk; I thought also that he might be a mugger,
and I prepared to defend myself or to strike. Just then another man
appeared; he, too, glared at me, but he took his friend by the arm
and tugged at him, saying it was not worth it. Reluctantly, the first
allowed himself to be led away. "Fucking Arab," he said.   20

    I am not, of course, an Arab. Nor am I, by nature, a gratuitously
belligerent chap. But my blood throbbed in my temples, and I called
out, "Say it to my face, coward, not as you run and hide." He stopped
where he was. I unlocked the boot, retrieving the tire iron from
where it lay; the cold metal of its shaft rested hungrily in my hands,   25
and I felt, at that moment, fully capable of wielding it with sufficient
violence to shatter the bones of his skull. We stood still for a few
murderous seconds; then my antagonist was once again pulled at,

---

1 **quantifiable**: sth. that can be measured or calculated and expressed in numbers
10 **tribe**: a group of people of the same race, and with the same customs, language,
religion, etc.   16 **mugger**: a person who threatens or attacks sb. in a public place in
order to steal their money   21 **gratuitous** [grəˈtjuːɪtəs]: done without any good
reason or purpose and often having harmful effects   22 **belligerent** [bəˈlɪdʒərənt]:
aggressive   **throb**: beat with a strong rhythm   **temple**: *Schläfe*   24 **boot**:
Kofferraum   **tire iron**: a metal tool for changing tires on a car   26 **wield sth.**: hold
sth. to use it as a weapon or tool   27 **shatter sth.**: break sth. into small pieces

and he departed muttering a string of obscenities. When I sat in my car my hands were unsteady; I have, in the uniforms of the various teams for which I have played, had my share of fights – but this encounter had an intensity that was for me unprecedented, and it
5 was some minutes before I deemed myself fit to drive.

What did he look like, you ask? Well, sir, he … But how odd! I cannot now recall the man's particulars, his age, say, or his build; to be honest, I cannot now recall many of the details of the events I have been relating to you. But surely it is the *gist* that matters; I am,
10 after all, telling you a history, and in history, as I suspect you – an American – will agree, it is the thrust of one's narrative that counts, not the accuracy of one's details. Still, I can assure you that everything I have told you thus far happened, for all intents and purposes, more or less as I have described.

15 In any case, let us not allow ourselves to be diverted. Some days after the incident in the parking lot – close to the end of our project at the cable company – I was again driving back to Manhattan with Jim. It was late, and we were both hungry; he suggested, as I was dropping him off, that he panfry us a pair of tuna steaks. His flat was
20 not the conservative, Upper East Side, liveried-doorman sort of place one might have expected; it was instead in TriBeCa, a four-thousand-square-foot loft that occupied the top floor of a nondescript building on Duane Street. Entering for the first time, I was struck by its *fashionable* quality, the sense it conveyed of attaching great value
25 to design. Not that it was cluttered, or indeed feminine in any way; no, if anything it was a minimalist affair with cement floors and pipes conspicuously fastened to the ceiling. But each piece of furniture seemed perfectly curated – lit and positioned just so – and

---

1 **a string of sth.**: a series of sth.   4 **unprecedented**: that has never happened before   5 **deem sth.** (fml): have a particular opinion about sth.   11 **thrust**: the main point of an argument, etc.   19 **tuna**: *Thunfisch*   20 **Upper East Side**: a wealthy neighborhood in Manhattan   **liveried**: wearing a type of uniform   22 **loft**: large one-room flat in a former factory   **nondescript**: having no interesting or unusual features or qualities   25 **cluttered with sth.**: full of sth. in a way that is untidy   27 **conspicuous** [kən'spɪkjuːəs]: easy to see or notice; likely to attract attention   28 **curated**: arranged in an organized manner

the walls featured impressive and forceful works of art, including, I realized, a not insignificant number of male nudes.

Jim rolled up his sleeves and asked, over the sizzle of our fish, what was on my mind. I sat at a stool, separated from him by the bar of his open-plan kitchen, which served also as a surface for dining. "Nothing, really," I said. "Is your family not at home?" He turned to me – visibly amused – and said, "I'm not married." "Ah," I said, "no children?" "No children," he affirmed, "but you're dodging my question." "What do you mean?" I asked. "You haven't been yourself lately," he said. "You're preoccupied. Something's eating at you. If I had to guess, I'd say it's your Pakistani side. You're worried about what's going on in the world." "No, no," I said, shaking my head to dismiss any possibility that my loyalties could be so divided, "things at home are a little unsettled, but it will pass." He seemed unconvinced. "Is your family okay?" he asked. "Yes," I said, "thank you." "All right then," he said, "but as I've told you before, I know what it's like to be an outsider. If you ever want to talk, give me a shout."

I left Jim's flat hoping I had thrown him off the scent. Still, my apparent transparency was alarming; Jim was a particularly perceptive observer, but if my internal conflicts were evident to him, then perhaps they were evident to others as well. I had heard tales of the discrimination Muslims were beginning to experience in the business world – stories of rescinded job offers and groundless dismissals – and I did not wish to have my position at Underwood Samson compromised. Besides, I knew that our firm, like much of our industry, had seen a sharp downturn in activity levels following the September attacks, and Wainwright had shared with me a rumor that cutbacks were on their way.

---

3 **sizzle**: noise made when sth. is fried   8 **dodge sth.**: avoid sth.   10 **eat (away) at sb.**: worry sb. over a period of time   19 **throw sb. off the scent**: do sth. to stop sb. from finding out about you   21 **perceptive**: having or showing the ability to see or understand things quickly   24 **rescind sth.** [ri'sɪnd] (fml): officially state that sth. (e.g. a law, contract) is no longer valid   **groundless**: without reason   25 **dismissal**: the act of firing sb. from their job   26 **compromise sb./sth.**: put sb./sth. into a difficult position   27 **downturn**: a fall in the amount of business that is done   29 **cutback**: a reduction in sth.

Our project at the cable company went on to end well – in the sense that we identified substantial cost savings and our client was pleased by the thoroughness of our valuation – but I was a nervous young man on the day of my December review. As it turned out,
5 I need not have been so concerned. Two of the six analysts in my entering class – those ranked fifth and sixth – were indeed among the employees our firm let go. But I, Jim informed me, was once again ranked number one; I was, in fact, awarded a prorated bonus that, although not enormous by the standards of our profession, was
10 still rather generous given the expectation of lean times ahead. It enabled me to pay off, in full, my outstanding student loans and put aside a few thousand as well. I should have been ecstatic, but earlier that week armed men had assaulted the Indian Parliament, and instead of celebrating my good fortune, I was confronting the
15 possibility that soon my country could be at war.

My mother told me not to come; my father said much the same. But with the help of a Seventh Avenue travel consolidator and my sudden ability to afford Business Plus class airfare on PIA, I found myself bound for Lahore at that time of year when New York
20 shoppers busy themselves with the purchasing of last-minute presents and couples can be seen kissing on the streets as they drag beautiful little shrubs to their apartments for use as Christmas trees. I sat on the airplane next to a man who removed his shoes – much to my dismay – and who said, after praying in the aisle, that nuclear
25 annihilation would not be avoided if it was God's will, but God's will in this matter was as yet unknown. He offered me a kindly smile, and I suspected that his purpose in making this remark was to reassure me.

And with that, sir, the moment has come for us to eat! For your
30 own safety, I would suggest that you avoid this yoghurt and those

---

8 **prorated**: *anteilig* 10 **lean**: difficult and not producing much money, etc.
13 **assault sb./sth.**: attack sb./sth. violently   17 **travel consolidator**: type of travel agency that can offer cheap tickets   18 **airfare**: the price you pay for a plane ticket
PIA: Pakistan International Airlines   24 **dismay**: a worried feeling after you have received an unpleasant surprise   25 **annihilation** [əˌnaɪəˈleɪʃən]: complete destruction   26 **kindly** (adj., old-fashioned): kind and caring

chopped vegetables. What? No, no, I meant nothing sinister; your stomach might be upset by uncooked foods, that is all. If you insist, I will go so far as to sample each of these plates myself first, to reassure you that there is nothing to fear. Here. A piece of warm bread, like so – ah, fresh from the clay oven – and I will begin. 5

1 **sinister**: evil, dangerous   2 **insist**: demand that sth. happens   3 **sample sth.**: test sth. by trying a little bit of it

9

Will they provide us with cutlery, you ask? I am certain, sir, that a fork can be found for you, but allow me to suggest that the time has now come for us to dirty our hands. We have, after all, spent some hours in each other's company already, surely you can no longer feel
5 the need to hold back. There is great satisfaction to be had in touching one's prey; indeed, millennia of evolution ensure that manipulating our meals with our skin heightens our sense of taste – and our appetite, for that matter! I see you need no further convincing; your fingers are tearing the flesh of that kebab with
10 considerable determination.

There are adjustments one must make if one comes here from America; a different way of *observing* is required. I recall the Americanness of my own gaze when I returned to Lahore that winter when war was in the offing. I was struck at first by how shabby our
15 house appeared, with cracks running through its ceilings and dry bubbles of paint flaking off where dampness had entered its walls. The electricity had gone that afternoon, giving the place a gloomy air, but even in the dim light of the hissing gas heaters our furniture appeared dated and in urgent need of reupholstery and repair. I was
20 saddened to find it in such a state – no, more than saddened, I was shamed. *This* was where I came from, this was my provenance, and it smacked of lowliness.

But as I reacclimatized and my surroundings once again became familiar, it occurred to me that the house had not changed in my
25 absence. *I* had changed; I was looking about me with the eyes of a foreigner, and not just any foreigner, but that particular type of

---

1 **cutlery**: *Besteck*   7 **heighten sth.** [ˈhaɪtən]: intensify sth.   11 **adjustment**: a change in the way a person behaves or thinks   14 **in the offing** (infml): likely to appear or happen soon   16 **flake off**: fall off in small thin pieces   **dampness**: *Feuchtigkeit*   21 **provenance** [ˈprɑːvənəns]: the place that sb./sth. originally came from   22 **smack of sth.**: seem to have sth. (esp. a particular unpleasant quality) **lowliness**: the state of being low in status, rank or importance

entitled and unsympathetic American who so annoyed me when I encountered him in the classrooms and workplaces of your country's elite. This realization angered me; staring at my reflection in the speckled glass of my bathroom mirror I resolved to exorcize the unwelcome sensibility by which I had become possessed.   5

It was only after so doing that I saw my house properly again, appreciating its enduring grandeur, its unmistakable personality and idiosyncratic charm. Mughal miniatures and ancient carpets graced its reception rooms; an excellent library abutted its veranda. It was far from impoverished; indeed, it was rich with history. I wondered   10 how I could ever have been so ungenerous – and so blind – to have thought otherwise, and I was disturbed by what this implied about myself: that I was a man lacking in substance and hence easily influenced by even a short sojourn in the company of others.

But far more significant than these inward-oriented musings of   15 mine was the external reality of the threat facing my home. My brother had come to collect me from the airport; he embraced me with sufficient force to cause my rib cage to flex. As he drove he ruffled my hair with his hand. I felt suddenly very young – or perhaps I felt my age: an almost childlike twenty-two, rather than   20 that permanent middle-age that attaches itself to the man who lives alone and supports himself by wearing a suit in a city not of his birth. It had been some time since I had been touched so easily, so familiarly, and I smiled. "How are things?" I asked him. He shrugged. "There is an artillery battery dug in at the country house of a friend   25 of mine, half an hour from here, and a colonel billeted in his spare bedroom," he replied, "so things are not good."

1 **entitled**: feeling that you have a right to the good things in life without necessarily having to work for them   4 **speckled**: covered with small marks or spots
exorcize sth. (fml): remove sth. that is bad or painful from your mind   7 **enduring**: lasting for a long time   8 **idiosyncratic** [ˌɪdiəʊsənˈkrætɪk]: eccentric   9 **abut sth.** [əˈbʌt] (fml): be next to sth. or to have one side touching the side of sth.
10 **impoverished**: very poor   14 **sojourn** [soʊˈdʒɜːrn]: temporary stay in a place away from your home   18 **rib cage**: *Brustkorb*   25 **artillery battery**: a number of large, heavy guns   26 **billet sb.**: *jdn. einquartieren*

My parents seemed well; they were more frail than when I had
seen them last, but at their age that was to be expected with the
passage of a year. My mother twirled a hundred-rupee note around
my head to bless my return; later it would be given to charity. My
5 father's eyes glistened, moist and brown. "Contact lenses," he said,
dabbing them with a handkerchief, "quite smart, eh?" I said they
suited him, and they did; his glasses had come late in life, and they
had concealed the strength of his face. Neither he nor my mother
wanted to discuss the possibility of war; they insisted on feeding me
10 and hearing in detail about my life in New York and my progress at
my new job. It was odd to speak of that world here, as it would be
odd to sing in a mosque; what is natural in one place can seem
unnatural in another, and some concepts travel rather poorly, if at
all. I censored any mention of Erica, for example, and indeed of
15 anything that I thought might disturb them.

But that night a family banquet was held in my honor, and there
the conflict with India dominated conversation. Opinion was
divided as to whether the men who had attacked the Indian
parliament had anything to do with Pakistan, but there was
20 unanimity in the belief that despite the assistance we had given
America in Afghanistan, America would not fight at our side. Already,
the Indian army was mobilizing, and Pakistan had begun to respond:
convoys of trucks, I was told, were passing through the city, bearing
supplies to our troops on the border; as we ate, we could hear the
25 sounds of military helicopters flying low overhead; a rumor
circulated that soon traffic would be halted on the motorway so that
our fighter planes could practice landing on it, in case all of our
airfields were destroyed in a nuclear exchange.

It will perhaps be odd for you – coming, as you do, from a
30 country that has not fought a war on its own soil in living memory,
the rare sneak attack or terrorist outrage excepted – to imagine

---

1 **frail**: physically weak and thin   3 **rupee**: the unit of money in Pakistan
4 **charity**: an organization that helps people in need   14 **censor sth.**: remove the
parts of sth. that are considered to be offensive or immoral   20 **unanimity**
[ˌjuːnəˈnɪməti]: complete agreement about sth. among a group of people   23 **bear
sth.**: carry sth.   30 **soil**: ground, territory   31 **sneak attack**: surprise attack

residing within commuting distance of a million or so hostile troops who could, at any moment, attempt a full-scale invasion. My brother cleaned his shotgun. One of my uncles stocked up on bottled water and canned food. Our part-time gardener was deployed with the reserves. But for the most part, people seemed to go about their lives 5 normally; Lahore was the last major city in a contiguous swath of Muslim lands stretching west as far as Morocco and had therefore that quality of understated bravado characteristic of frontier towns.

But I worried. I felt powerless; I was angry at our weakness, at our vulnerability to intimidation of this sort from our – admittedly 10 much larger – neighbor to the east. Yes, we had nuclear weapons, and yes, our soldiers would not back down, but we were being threatened nonetheless, and there was nothing I could do about it but lie in my bed, unable to sleep. Indeed, I would soon be gone, leaving my family and my home behind, and this made me a kind of 15 coward in my own eyes, a traitor. What sort of man abandons his people in such circumstances? And what was I abandoning them for? A well-paying job and a woman whom I longed for but who refused even to see me? I grappled with these questions again and again. 20

When the time came for me to return to New York I told my parents I wanted to stay longer, but they would not hear of it. Perhaps they sensed that I was myself divided, that something called me back to America; perhaps they were simply protecting their son. "Do not forget to shave before you go," my mother said to me. 25 "Why?" I asked, indicating my father and brother. "They have beards." "They," she replied, "have them only because they wish to hide the fact that they are bald. Besides, you are still a boy." She stroked my stubble with her fingers and added, "It makes you look like a mouse." 30

---

3 **stock up on sth.**: buy a lot of sth. so that you can use it later   4 **deploy sb./sth.**: move sb./sth (e.g. soldiers or weapons) into a position where they are ready for military action   6–7 **swath of land**: *Landstrich, Schneise*   8 **bravado**: *Wagemut*
10 **vulnerability**: the condition of being weak and easily hurt   **intimidation**: the action of frightening or threatening sb. so that they will do what you want
16 **traitor**: *Verräter/in*   19 **grapple with sth.**: try hard to find a solution to sth. (e.g. a problem)   26 **indicate sb./sth.** (fml): point at sb./sth.   28 **bald**: *glatzköpfig, kahl*

On the flight I noticed how many of my fellow passengers were similar to me in age: college students and young professionals, heading back after the holidays. I found it ironic; children and the elderly were meant to be sent away from impending battles, but in
5 our case it was the fittest and brightest who were leaving, those who in the past would have been most expected to remain. I was filled with contempt for myself, such contempt that I could not bring myself to converse or to eat. I shut my eyes and waited, and the hours took from me the responsibility even to flee.
10 You are not unfamiliar with the anxieties that precede armed conflict, you say? Aha! Then you have been in the service, sir, just as I suspected! Would you not agree that waiting for what is to come is the most difficult part? Yes, quite so, not as difficult as the time of carnage itself – said, sir, like a true soldier. But I see that you have
15 paused in your eating; perhaps you are waiting for fresh bread. Here, have half of mine. No, I insist; our waiter will bring us more momentarily.

Given your background, you will doubtless have experienced the peculiar phenomenon that is the return to an environment more or
20 less at peace from one where the prospect of large-scale bloodshed is a distinct possibility. It is an odd transition. My colleagues greeted with consternation my reappearance in our offices. For despite my mother's request, and my knowledge of the difficulties it could well present me at immigration, I had not shaved my two-week-old
25 beard. It was, perhaps, a form of protest on my part, a symbol of my identity, or perhaps I sought to remind myself of the reality I had just left behind; I do not now recall my precise motivations. I know only that I did not wish to blend in with the army of clean-shaven youngsters who were my co-workers, and that inside me, for
30 multiple reasons, I was deeply angry.

It is remarkable, given its physical insignificance – it is only a hairstyle, after all – the impact a beard worn by a man of my

7 **contempt**: *Verachtung*   8 **converse with sb.** (fml): have a conversation with sb.
10 **precede sb./sth.** (fml): happen before sth. or come before sth./sb. in order
14 **carnage** [ˈkɑːrnɪdʒ]: the violent killing of a large number of people
20 **prospect** of sth./of doing sth.: the possibility that sth. will happen   28 **blend in with sb./sth.**: become similar to or match sth. (e.g. your surroundings)

complexion has on your fellow countrymen. More than once, traveling on the subway – where I had always had the feeling of seamlessly blending in – I was subjected to verbal abuse by complete strangers, and at Underwood Samson I seemed to become overnight a subject of whispers and stares. Wainwright tried to offer me some friendly advice. "Look, man," he said, "I don't know what's up with the beard, but I don't think it's making you Mister Popular around here." "They are common where I come from," I told him. "Jerk chicken is common where I come from," he replied, "but I don't smear it all over my face. You need to be careful. This whole corporate collegiality veneer only goes so deep. Believe me."

I appreciated my friend's concern, but I did not take his suggestion. Despite the layoffs, the utilization rate at our firm remained low in January, and I sat at my desk with little to do. I spent this time online, reading about the ongoing deterioration of affairs between India and Pakistan, the assessment by experts of the military balance in the region and likely scenarios for battle, and the negative impact the standoff was already beginning to have on the economies of both nations. I wondered how it was that America was able to wreak such havoc in the world – orchestrating an entire war in Afghanistan, say, and legitimizing through its actions the invasion of weaker states by more powerful ones, which India was now proposing to do to Pakistan – with so few apparent consequences at home.

I also, after six weeks of attempting not to communicate with her, finally called Erica, and because her phone was constantly off, followed up by sending an email. I would like to claim my message was brief, a polite hello that was for the most part respectful of her request for silence, but in truth I spent many hours composing it

---

3 **seamless**: *nahtlos*   **subject sb./sth. to sth.**: make sb./sth. experience sth unpleasant   **abuse**: insults   8–9 **jerk chicken** type of spicy Jamaican chicken dish   11 **veneer** [vəˈnɪr] (fml): an outer appearance of a particular quality that hides the true nature of sb./sth.   13 **layoff**: an act of making people unemployed because there is no work for them to do   **utilization rate**: *Auslastungsrate* 15 **deterioration** [dɪˌtɪriəˈreɪʃən]: process of becoming worse   18 **standoff**: a situation in which no agreement can be reached   20 **wreak havoc** (fml): do great damage or harm

and it was perhaps the lengthiest I have ever written. In it I told her
of what had been happening in my life, both at work and at home,
and the turmoil through which I was passing; I also told her how
much I missed her and that I did not understand where or why she
5 had gone. It was some days before she replied. "I'm at a sort of
clinic," she wrote, "an institution where people can recover
themselves. I think of you, too." She invited me to come and visit
her; it would be easier for her to attempt to answer my questions
face-to-face.

10   The clinic was an afternoon's drive from the city, a converted villa
set in fifty acres of secluded countryside overlooking the Hudson
River. I was greeted by a nurse in the reception area. "You must be
Changez," she said. "Erica has told me a lot about you." "I am,"
I said. "How did you know?" "Eyelashes like a Maybelline ad," she
15 replied, "that's what she said." As I considered this unlikely
description, the nurse explained that Erica had been waiting for me
but became a little nervous and went for a walk, asking the nurse to
explain a few things on her behalf. "So she will not see me?" I asked.
The nurse smiled. "Sure she will, honey," she said, "but people get
20 embarrassed sometimes when they're in a place like this. She thinks
it won't be as awkward for you both if I talk to you first." She patted
my hand. Then she added, "I'm like the shower you take before you
jump into a swimming pool."

What I had to understand about Erica, the nurse told me, was
25 that she was in love with someone else. She knew it would be tough
for me to hear, but I had to hear it regardless. It did not matter that
the person Erica was in love with was what the nurse or I might call
deceased; for Erica he was alive enough, and that was the problem:
it was difficult for Erica to be out in the world, living the way the
30 nurse or I might, when in her mind she was experiencing things that
were stronger and more meaningful than the things she could
experience with the rest of us. So Erica felt better in a place like this,

---

3 **turmoil**: a state of great anxiety and confusion   10 **converted**: be changed from
one use to another use   11 **secluded**: quiet and private   14 **Maybelline**: brand
name of a make-up company   21 **awkward** [ˈɔːkwərd]: *peinlich, unangenehm*
26 **regardless**: nevertheless

separated from the rest of us, where people could live in their minds without feeling bad about it. "But eventually she will have to leave here," I said. "Perhaps she will want to be with me then." The nurse shook her head. "Maybe," she said, "but right now you're the hardest person for her to see. You're the one who upsets her most. Because 5 you're the most real, and you make her lose her balance."

The nurse suggested I was likely to find Erica at the end of a path that wound through the wooded grounds, in a small copse on a hilltop. She was indeed there, sitting on a bench of rough-hewn timber. She wore a heavy jacket and turned at my approach; she was 10 gaunt, her flesh seeming almost bruised where it passed over the bones of her face, and she glowed with something not unlike the fervor of the *devout*. She extended her hand, but instead of shaking it I kissed it, my lips touching the synthetic polymers of her winter glove. She smiled. "You look cute," she said. "Your beard brings out 15 your eyes." I thought she looked like someone who was about to complete the month of fasting and had been too consumed by prayer and reading of the holy book to give sufficient thought to the nightly meal, but I did not say so.

She offered me her arm and we strolled together, speaking softly; 20 the mist of our breathing preceded us. "This is a good place for me right now," she said. "I feel calm here." "You seem calm," I said, resisting the urge to add, *too calm*. "I'm sorry I've been hiding," she said. "It's not that I haven't wanted to see you. It's just that I could see I was pulling you in, and I didn't want you to get hurt. I thought it 25 would be better for you like this." "Why would I get hurt?" I asked. "It hurts when you care about someone and they go away," she replied. "But where are you going?" I asked. She shrugged and did not answer.

We walked on in silence but for the sound of snow crunching 30 under our feet; my ears began to ache from the cold. "Do you write here?" I asked. "No," she said, "not in the sense of putting stuff

8 **copse**: a small area of trees or bushes growing together   9 **rough-hewn**: *grob gehauen*   11 **gaunt**: very thin, usu. because of illness, hunger or worry   13 **fervor**: very strong feelings about sth.   **devout**: a person who believes strongly in a particular religion   23 **urge**: a strong desire

down. But I think a lot. I imagine." "And do I sometimes figure in your imaginings?" I asked. "Sometimes," she said, smiling. "Any fantasies of kinky sex," I said, "with an exotic foreigner given to role-playing?" She laughed and squeezed my arm; for the first time her
5 face seemed to soften, to become almost vulnerable. But then she again receded inside herself. "You helped me," she said. "You were kind and true, and I'm grateful."

It was the certainty with which she placed me in the past tense that struck me most about her statement. I felt hope being quenched
10 within me, and although I said, "Do not be grateful, be lustful – come back to New York with me," I said it without that core of conviction that gives words their power; she leaned her head momentarily against my shoulder, but she was not compelled to respond. I watched her out of the corner of my eye as we made our
15 way to the main building together, wondering how much of her detached and seemingly ascetic state was a consequence of the medication she was consuming. For a moment, I was seized by the wild notion of abducting her and taking her away with me in my rental car; surely my ministrations would be more productive in
20 restoring her to reality than the chemicals she was subjecting herself to here. But the absurdity – and disrespect to her – of such an act was immediately obvious to me, and I did nothing of the sort.

"Do you know how to ski?" she asked me. "No," I said, "I have never been." "Chris and I," she said, "used to go every winter –
25 Colorado, usually, or once in a while Vermont. We even did a little cross-country together in Central Park, when we were kids. We each got a pair as a present and we snuck out with them without telling anyone. We got into trouble. Our parents called the police. It was fun, though. Anyway, this place reminds me of that. Especially the
30 snow on that slope. It's so gentle and it seems so soft. You should go sometime." We had reached the gravel of the driveway. "You should

---

1 **figure in sth.**: play a role/part in sth.   3 **kinky**: (of sex) strange or unusual
5 **vulnerable**: weak and easily hurt   7 **grateful**: thankful   9 **quench sth.**: *etwas erlöschen*   11–12 **core of conviction**: *im Brustton der Überzeugung*   18 **abduct sb.**: kidnap sb.   19 **ministrations** (pl, fml): the act of helping or caring for sb.
27 **sneak out** (infml): go somewhere secretly   31 **gravel**: small stones, often used to make the surface of paths and roads

take me," I said. She shook her head. "I can't," she said, "but you should still go. Try to be happy, okay? I'm sorry about everything. Please take care of yourself."

She gave me a hug and afterwards she stood there, looking at me. But he is *dead,* I wanted to shout! It was all I could do not to kiss her 5 then; perhaps I should have. I had to choose whether to continue to try to win her over or to accept her wishes and leave, and in the end I chose the latter. Maybe, I told myself as I drove away, it was a test and I failed; maybe I should have risked it. I almost turned around and went back, but in the end I did not do so. Things might have 10 worked out rather differently if I had turned around; then again, things might have worked out exactly the same.

I cut a desolate figure in the office after that, angry and preoccupied with thoughts of Erica and of home. I was negligent at my administrative duties, and did absolutely nothing to seek out a 15 new assignment for myself. I half expected someone to come to my desk with a pink slip to put me out of my misery. Instead, Jim summoned me to issue a surprising stamp of approval. "Listen, kid," he said, "some people around here think you're looking kind of shabby. The beard and all. Quite frankly, I don't give a shit. Your 20 performance is what counts, as far as I'm concerned, and you're the best analyst in your class by a long way. Besides, I know it must be tough for you with what's going on in Pakistan. What you need is to get yourself busy, which I'll admit isn't easy when we have as dry a pipeline as we do right now. But I've got a new project, valuing a 25 book publisher in Valparaiso, Chile. It's going to have to be a small team, just a vice president and an analyst. Normally, I'd offer it to someone with more experience. But I'm offering it to you. What do you think?" "Thank you, sir," I muttered. He laughed. "A bit of enthusiasm, please," he said, adding, "It's a lot of responsibility. 30 There won't be any backup for you." "You can rely on me," I said,

---

13 **desolate**: very lonely and unhappy   17 **pink slip** (AE infml): a letter given to
sb. to say that they must leave their job   18 **stamp of approval**: *offene Zustimmung*
31 **backup**: support

this time with what I hoped was greater apparent sincerity. I do not know if I succeeded, however, because although Jim smiled in response, his expression was one of puzzlement.

But I observe that you, sir, have stopped eating. Can it be that
5 you are full? Very well, I will not insist; I will, however, order us some dessert, a little rice pudding with sliced almonds and cardamom, the perfect sweetener for an evening such as ours, which is taking a turn towards the grimmer side. Such dishes may not normally be to your taste, but I would encourage you to have, at the
10 very least, a tiny bite. After all, one reads that the soldiers of your country are sent to battle with chocolate in their rations, so the prospect of sugaring your tongue before undertaking even the bloodiest of tasks cannot be entirely alien to you.

13 **alien**: unknown, unfamiliar

10

When you sit in that fashion, sir, with your arm curved around the back of the empty chair beside you, a bulge manifests itself through the lightweight fabric of your suit, precisely at that point parallel to the sternum where the undercover security agents of our country – and indeed, one assumes, of all countries – tend to favor wearing an   5 armpit holster for their sidearm. No, no, please do not adjust your position on my account! I did not mean to imply that you were so equipped; I am certain that in your case it is merely the outline of one of those travel wallets in which the prudent secrete their possessions so that they are less likely to be discovered by thieves.   10

I myself employed no such precautions on my trip to Chile. We again flew in the relative comfort of first class, but I was no longer excited by the luxuries of our cabin; unlike Jim, who was as usual accompanying us for the commencement of the project, and the vice president who would be my immediate commanding officer for the   15 full duration of this tour, I turned down our flight attendant's many offers of champagne. For all the hours that we were airborne, I neither ate nor slept; my thoughts were caught up in the affairs of continents other than the one below us, and more than once I regretted coming at all.   20

I wondered what I could do to help Erica. Seeing her as I had seen her last – emaciated, detached, and so lacking in *life* – pained me; I recalled the dog we had had in my childhood and his passivity and desire for solitude in those last days before he succumbed to the

---

2 **bulge** [bʌldʒ]: a lump that sticks out from sth. in a round shape   4 **sternum**: *Brustbein*   6 **sidearm**: a weapon (usu. a revolver) worn at the side   9 **prudent** (n): a sensible and careful person   **secrete sth. in sth.** [sɪˈkriːt] (fml): hide sth. small 11 **precaution**: sth. that is done in advance in order to prevent problems or to avoid danger   14 **commencement** (fml): beginning   16 **duration** (fml): length of time that sth. lasts   17 **airborne**: in the air   22 **emaciated** [iˈmeɪʃieɪtəd]: thin and weak, usu. due to illness or hunger   24 **succumb to sth.** [səˈkʌm]: not be able to fight sth. (e.g. an attack or an illness)

leukemia induced in him by that brand of tick powder a veterinarian
would subsequently tell us never to use. But Erica was not suffering
from leukemia; there was no physical reason for her malaise beyond,
perhaps, a biochemical disposition towards mental disorders of this
5 kind. No, hers was an illness of the spirit, and I had been raised in
an environment too thoroughly permeated with a tradition of shared
rituals of mysticism to accept that conditions of the spirit could not
be influenced by the care, affection, and desire of others. What was
essential was that I seek to understand why I had failed to penetrate
10 the membrane with which she guarded her psyche; my more direct
approaches had been rejected, but with sufficient insight I might yet
be welcomed through a process of osmosis. I could imagine no
alternative but to try; my longing for her was undiminished despite
our months of near-complete separation.

15 It was in such a frame of mind that I arrived in Santiago. We
traveled from there by road – making good progress except for a
brief blockage where the mechanical shovels of repair crews tore out
great bites of the red earth that characterizes Chile's central valley –
and we smelled our destination before we saw it; Valparaiso lay on
20 the briny Pacific and was hidden from view by a crest of hills.

The chief of the publishing company was an old man by the
name of Juan-Bautista, given to smoking unfiltered cigarettes and
sporting glasses thick enough to burn through paper on a sunny day.
He reminded me of my maternal grandfather; I liked him at once.
25 "What do you know of books?" he asked us. "I specialize in the
media industry," Jim replied. "I've valued a dozen publishers over
two decades." "That is finance," Juan-Bautista retorted. "I asked what
you knew of books." "My father's uncle was a poet," I found myself
saying. "He was well-known in the Punjab. Books are loved in my
30 family." Juan-Bautista looked at me as though becoming aware of the

---

1 **tick**: *Zecke*   6 **permeate sth.**: affect all levels or areas of sth.   11 **sufficient**:
enough   12 **osmosis**: the gradual process of learning or being influenced by sth.,
as a result of being in close contact with it   15 **frame**: state, condition
19 **Valparaiso**: Chile's third largest metropolitan city and its most important port
20 **briny**: salty   23 **sport sth.**: wear sth. in a proud way   24 **maternal**: related
through the mother's side of the family   27 **retort**: reply quickly to a comment in
an angry or humorous way

presence of this youngster before him for the first time; I did not speak in that meeting again.

Jim explained to us afterwards that Juan-Bautista was not pleased to have us there. Although he had run the company for many years, he did not own it; the owners wanted to sell, and the prospective   5
buyer – our client – was unlikely to continue to subsidize the loss-making trade division with income from the profitable educational and professional publishing arms. Trade, with its stable of literary – defined for all practical purposes as commercially unviable – authors was a drag on the rest of the enterprise; our task was to determine   10
the value of the asset if that drag were shut down.

We set ourselves up in a handsome, if aging, conference room with a large oval table and bookshelves lining the walls. When a strong breeze blew, I could hear outside our windows the clicking of wooden storm shutters against their restraints. It was hot during the   15
afternoons – we had come during the southern summer – but sometimes we would wake to fog and a morning chill, and in those moments I was glad for the wool of my suit. Jim left after two days, remarking in my presence to the vice president that he could expect impressive things of me. But although my laptop was open, my   20
Internet connection enabled, and my pen and notebook positioned by my side – I found myself unable to concentrate on our work.

Instead I perused news websites which informed me that Pakistan and India were conducting tit-for-tat tests of their ballistic missiles and that a stream of foreign dignitaries was visiting the capitals of   25
both countries, urging Delhi to desist from its warlike rhetoric and Islamabad to make concessions that would enable a retreat from the

---

5 **prospective**: potential   6 **subsidize sth.**: support sth. financially   7 **trade division**: *Handelssparte*   8 **arm**: a section of a large organization that deals with one particular activity   9 **unviable** [ʌn'vaɪəbəl]: not capable of surviving   10 **drag** (infml): a person or thing that makes progress difficult   11 **asset**: *Vermögenswert*   17 **chill**: a feeling of being cold   23 **peruse sth.** [pə'ruːz] (fml): read sth., esp. in a careful way   24 **tit-for-tat**: a situation in which you do sth. bad to sb. because they have done the same to you   **ballistic missile**: *Raketengeschoss*   25 **dignitary**: a person who has an important official position   26, 27 **Delhi, Islamabad**: the capitals of India and Pakistan respectively   26 **desist from sth.** (fml): stop doing sth.   27 **concession**: *Zugeständnis*

brink of catastrophe. I wondered, sir, about your country's role in all this: surely, with American bases already established in Pakistan for the conduct of the Afghanistan campaign, all America would have to do would be to inform India that an attack on Pakistan would be
5   treated as an attack on any American ally and would be responded to by the overwhelming force of America's military. Yet your country was signally failing to do this; indeed, America was maintaining a strict neutrality between the two potential combatants, a position that favored, of course, the larger and – at that moment in history –
10 the more belligerent of them.

These thoughts preoccupied me when I should have been gathering data and building my financial model. Moreover, Valparaiso was itself a distraction: the city was powerfully atmospheric; a sense of melancholy pervaded its boulevards and
15 hillsides. I read online about its history and discovered that it had been in decline for over a century; once a great port fought over by rivals because of its status as the last stop for vessels making their way from the Pacific to the Atlantic, it had been bypassed and rendered peripheral by the Panama Canal. In this – Valparaiso's
20 former aspirations to grandeur – I was reminded of Lahore and of that saying, so evocative in our language: *the ruins proclaim the building was beautiful.*

I sensed the vice president was growing increasingly irritated with me; I could hardly blame him: he was working from morning
25 until midnight, poor fellow, with little support from his only teammate. I pretended to be keeping myself busy, but as the days passed and my deadlines began to slip, he lost patience. "Look, man," he said, "what's the problem? You're not getting anything

---

1 **brink**: *Schwelle*   7 **signally**: in a way that is serious and very noticeable
maintain sth.: make sth. continue at the same level, standard, etc.   8 **combatant**
['kɔmbətənt]: a person or group involved in fighting in a war or battle   17 **vessel**
(fml): a large ship or boat   18 **bypass sth.**: go around or avoid sth.   19 **render sb./**
sth. peripheral: *etwas zur Nebensache machen, etwas an den Rand drängen*
20 **aspiration**: a strong desire to have sth. better   **grandeur** ['grændʒər]: the
quality of being great and impressive in appearance   21 **evocative**: making you
think of or remember a strong image or feeling in a pleasant way   **proclaim sth.**
(fml): tell people about sth. important   27 **slip**: pass quickly or easily away

done. I know you're supposed to be good, but from my perspective, you aren't delivering squat. Tell me what you need. You want help with your model, more direction? Tell me and I'll give it to you, but for God's sake pull it together." He was a manager of excellent repute, and I might have considered revealing to him the turmoil taking 5 place inside me, but at the level of human beings our connection was nil. So I apologized, saying that his feedback had hit the mark, but that he need not worry because I would redouble my efforts. "Everything," I said, mustering a tone of maximum reassurance, "is under control." 10

For a time this appeared to satisfy him, although it was patently untrue. Yet I knew he had begun to resent me – and rightly so, after all: by not performing to plan I was making him look bad – and for my part I was beginning to resent him as well. I could not respect how he functioned so completely immersed in the structures of his 15 professional micro-universe. Yes, I too had previously derived comfort from my firm's exhortations to focus intensely on work, but now I saw that in this constant striving to realize a financial future, no thought was given to the critical personal and political issues that affect one's emotional present. In other words, my blinders were 20 coming off, and I was dazzled and rendered immobile by the sudden broadening of my arc of vision.

I noticed Juan-Bautista watching me as I shuffled about half-heartedly from one meeting to another. He kept his door open and his desk was positioned in such a way that it was possible for him to 25 gaze down the corridor. Once, as I was passing by, he called me to him. "I have," he said, "looked into this matter of the contemporary poets of the Punjab. Tell me, what was the name of your father's uncle?" I told him and he nodded; he had indeed seen him mentioned in an anthology available in Spanish translation. I was 30

---

2 **not be delivering squat** (sl): not showing results   4 **repute** (n, fml): reputation
7 **nil**: zero, nothing   8 **redouble sth.**: increase sth. or make it stronger
11 **patently** (fml): without doubt, clearly   12 **resent sb./sth.**: feel bitter or angry about sth.   16 **derive sth. from sth.** (fml): get sth. from sth.   17 **exhortation** [ˌegzɔːrˈteɪʃən]: *Ermahnung*   18 **striving** (n): the action of trying very hard to achieve sth.   23 **shuffle about**: walk slowly without lifting your feet completely off the ground

surprised and pleased to hear that this was the case, but before I
could respond he went on to say, "You seem very unlike your
colleagues. You appear somewhat lost." "Not at all," I replied, taken
aback. Then I added, "Although I must say I am quite moved by
5 Valparaiso." He suggested that I visit the house of Pablo Neruda, but
to go during the day as it was shut in the evening, and with that our
brief conversation concluded.

I never came to know why Juan-Bautista singled me out. Perhaps
he was gifted with remarkable powers of empathy and had observed
10 in me a dilemma that out of compassion he thought he could help
me resolve; perhaps he saw among his enemies one who was weak
and could easily be brought down; perhaps it was mere coincidence.
Sentimentally, I would like to believe in the first of these possibilities.
But regardless, Juan-Bautista added considerable momentum to my
15 inflective journey, a journey that continues to this day...

But I am getting ahead of myself, and in any case our dessert has
arrived. He has brought only a single bowl; I sensed that you were
not keen on having more than a taste, and the same is true of myself,
as I am now quite full. What do you think, sir? Ah, that puckering of
20 your lips is an inauspicious sign. Too sweet, you say? An interesting
observation, given that I have always felt your country to be rather
similar to mine in the intensity of its national desire for sweetness.
But perhaps you are atypical; your travels have taken you far from
the ubiquitous soda fountains and ice-cream bars of your
25 motherland.

I too had traveled far that January, but the home of Neruda did
not feel as removed from Lahore as it actually was; geographically, of

---

3–4 **be taken aback by sb./sth.**: be shocked or surprised by sb./sth.   5 **Pablo
Neruda** (1904–1973): Chilean poet, diplomat and politician, winner of the 1972
Nobe Prize for Literature   8 **single sb./sth. out**: choose sb./sth. from a group for
special attention   9 **gifted**: having a lot of natural ability or intelligence   **empathy**:
the ability to understand another person's feelings, experience, etc   10 **compassion**:
Mitleid   14 **considerable** (fml): great in amount, size, importance, etc.
14 **momentum**: *Schwung, Dynamik*   15 **inflective**: (here) ever changing
19–20 **pucker your lips**: *den Mund verziehen, die Lippen spitzen*   20 **inauspicious**
[ˌɪnɑːˈspɪʃəs] (fml): showing signs that the future will not be good or successful
24 **ubiquitous** [juˈbɪkwɪtəs]: seeming to be everywhere   24 **soda fountain**
(old-fashioned): type of bar where you can buy soft drinks, ice creams, etc.

course, it was perhaps as remote a place as could be found on the planet, but in spirit it seemed only an imaginary caravan ride away from my city, or a sail by night down the Ravi and Indus. I told the vice president that I was going out to inspect a distribution center and with this excuse made my way up into the hills, climbing higher 5
and higher, until when I turned to look at the ocean I saw gulls soaring at the same altitude as myself. The neighborhood was a poor one, with colorful murals like graffiti on the walls and children racing by on wooden carts that appeared to be shipping crates to which wheels had been attached. The house itself was compact and 10
beautiful, reminiscent of a boat jutting out over the bay; a garden cascaded below it, and behind the bar was a convex mirror, which Neruda had employed to convince his guests that they were drunk. I lingered on the terrace and watched the sun dip lower in the sky. In the distance, someone was playing the guitar; it was a delicate 15
melody, a song with no words.

I thought of Erica. It occurred to me that my attempts to communicate with her might have failed in part because I did not know where I stood on so many issues of consequence; I lacked a stable *core*. I was not certain where I belonged – in New York, in 20
Lahore, in both, in neither – and for this reason, when she reached out to me for help, I had nothing of substance to give her. Probably this was why I had been willing to try to take on the persona of Chris, because my own identity was so fragile. But in so doing – and by being unable to offer her an alternative to the chronic nostalgia 25
inside her – I might have pushed Erica deeper into her own confusion. I resolved to write this to her in an email, as a sort of apology, perhaps, and as an invitation to resume the contact between us that she had all but severed, and I recall pressing send without rereading even once what I had written. 30

---

1 **remote**: far away, isolated   3 **Ravi, Indus**: rivers that flow through Pakistan
8 **mural**: wall painting on the outside of a building   9 **crate**: a wooden container
for transporting goods   20 **core**: *Innerstes, Kern*   24 **fragile**: easily broken or
damaged   25 **chronic**: difficult to cure or get rid of   29 **sever sth.** [sevər]: break
off sth.

But days passed without any response, and I began to lose hope that one would come. I telephoned my parents and they told me that the situation in Pakistan continued to be precarious; it was rumored that India was acting with America's connivance, both countries
5 seeking through the threat of force to coerce our government into changing its policies. Moreover, our house's main water connection had ruptured – the pipes were long overdue for replacement – and the pressure was now so low that it had become impossible to take a shower; they were making do with buckets and ladles instead. This
10 caused me to reflect again on the absurdity of my situation, being two hemispheres – if such a thing is possible – from home at a time when my family was in need.

The only manner in which I could be of aid to them at that moment was to provide money, and this I did, wiring what little
15 savings I possessed to my brother because my father refused to accept it. The act of calling my bank to arrange the transfer ought to have impressed upon me the importance of my job: after all, I had no other source of income to fall back on. But instead my indifference to my work continued unabated. There was no longer any possibility
20 of deceiving the vice president; my lapses had become obvious, and his reprimands grew increasingly blunt. I wonder in retrospect why he did not reach out to Jim at that stage to have me replaced, but then again, this was not entirely surprising: the task of a vice president at our firm – the word vice in the title notwithstanding –
25 was to be as close to autonomous as possible. A good vice president was one who *got things done,* no matter what, and to appeal for assistance prematurely would be to undermine one's superior's confidence in one's abilities.

---

3 **precarious**: not safe or stable   4 **connivance** [kə'naɪvəns]: *stillschweigende Duldung, heimliches Einverständnis*   5 **coerce sb. into doing sth.** [koʊ'ɜːs] (fml): force sb. to do sth. by using threats   7 **rupture** (fml): break or burst open
9 **ladle** [leɪdəl]: large deep spoon with a long handle   14 **wire sth. to sb.**: send sth. (esp. money) from your bank to sb'. else's bank using an electronic system
19 **unabated** (fml): without becoming any less strong   21 **reprimand**: a severe form of criticism for a fault   27 **premature**: too early   **undermine sb./sth.**: make sb./sth. weaker or less effective

As for myself, I was clearly on the threshold of great change; only the final catalyst was now required, and in my case that catalyst took the form of lunch. Juan-Bautista's invitation caught me off guard; he simply mentioned, as I was passing his office one day, that it would be a shame to have visited Valparaiso without having tasted sea bass ⁵ cooked in salt, and as he intended to go to his favorite restaurant that afternoon, I really ought – if I were free – to accompany him. I said – out of politeness and curiosity, and also because I was eager to seize any pretext to avoid returning to the poisonous atmosphere of our team room – that it would be an honor, and the next thing I ¹⁰ knew, I found myself making my way through the streets of the city with a man who desired more than any other to see our client's acquisition fail to proceed.

Juan-Bautista wore a hat and carried a walking stick, and he ambled at a pace so slow that it would likely have been illegal for ¹⁵ him to cross at an intersection in New York. When we were seated and he had ordered on our behalf, he said, "I have been observing you, and I think it is no exaggeration to say, young man, that you seem upset. May I ask you a rather personal question?" "Certainly," I said. "Does it trouble you," he inquired, "to make your living by ²⁰ disrupting the lives of others?" "We just value," I replied. "We do not decide whether to buy or to sell, or indeed what happens to a company after we have valued it." He nodded; he lit a cigarette and took a sip from his glass of wine. Then he asked, "Have you heard of the janissaries?" "No," I said. "They were Christian boys," he ²⁵ explained, "captured by the Ottomans and trained to be soldiers in a Muslim army, at that time the greatest army in the world. They were ferocious and utterly loyal: they had fought to erase their own civilizations, so they had nothing else to turn to."

He tipped the ash of his cigarette onto a plate. "How old were you ³⁰ when you went to America?" he asked. "I went for college," I said.

---

2 **catalyst**: a person or thing that causes a change   3 **off guard**: not prepared for sth.   5 **sea bass**: *Zackenbarsch*   9 **pretext**: a false reason given for doing sth.   15 **amble**: walk at a slow relaxed speed   26 **Ottoman**: citizen or official of the Ottoman (Turkish) Empire, which lasted from 1299 to 1923   28 **ferocious**: very strong and aggressive

"I was eighteen." "Ah, much older," he said. "The janissaries were always taken in childhood. It would have been far more difficult to devote themselves to their adopted empire, you see, if they had memories they could not forget." He smiled and speculated no
5 further on the subject. Our food arrived shortly thereafter and the sea bass may well have been as splendid as he had claimed; unfortunately, I can no longer recall its taste.

But your expression, sir, tells me that you think something is amiss. Did this conversation really happen, you ask? For that matter,
10 did this so-called Juan-Bautista even exist? I assure you, sir: you can trust me. I am not in the habit of inventing untruths! And moreover, even if I were, there is no reason why this incident would be more likely to be false than any of the others I have related to you. Come, come, I believe we have passed through too much together to begin
15 to raise questions of this nature at so late a stage.

In any case, Juan-Bautista's words plunged me into a deep bout of introspection. I spent that night considering what I had become. There really could be no doubt: I was a modern-day janissary, a servant of the American empire at a time when it was invading a
20 country with a kinship to mine and was perhaps even colluding to ensure that my own country faced the threat of war. Of course I was struggling! Of course I felt torn! I had thrown in my lot with the men of Underwood Samson, with the officers of the empire, when all along I was predisposed to feel compassion for those, like Juan-
25 Bautista, whose lives the empire thought nothing of overturning for its own gain.

In the morning, with the demeanor of a man facing a firing squad – no, that is perhaps too dramatic, and a dangerous comparison on this of all evenings, but you understand my intent –

---

3 **devote yourself to sb./sth.**: give most of your time, energy, etc. to sb./sth.
9 **amiss** (adj): wrong; not as it should be   16 **plunge sb./sth. into sth.**: make sb./ sth. move suddenly forwards and/or downwards into sth.   17 **introspection**: the careful examination of your own thoughts and feelings   20 **kinship**: feeling of being close to sb. because you have a similar culture, etc. **collude with sb. in sth.** (fml): work together with sb. secretly in order to achieve sth.   22 **lot** (n): destiny, future   24 **predisposed**: *prädisponiert, empf*änglich   27–28 **firing squad**: *Exekutionskommando*   29 **intent** (fml): intention

I told the vice president that I refused to work any further. He was baffled. "What do you mean, refuse?" he said. "I am done here," I replied. "I intend to return to New York." Panic ensued; a conference call with Jim was hastily arranged. "Look, kid," an uncharacteristically tense Jim said over the speakerphone, "I know you have stuff on 5 your mind. But if you walk out on this now you undermine our firm. You hurt your team. In wartime soldiers don't really fight for their flags, Changez. They fight for their friends, their buddies. Their team. Well, right now your team is asking you to stay. Afterwards, if you need a break, it's yours." 10

I must admit, Jim's words gave me pause. I had great admiration for him; he had always stood by me, and now I proposed to betray him. By the time my replacement could be dispatched and brought up to speed, it was probable that the deadline for our valuation would be missed. Jim had sent me as an act of faith and generosity; 15 my repayment would be a slap in the face and all the more impudent for coming at a time of financial weakness for the firm. Besides, without my job – which I was certain to lose – my visa would expire, and I would be compelled to leave the United States. But I resolved not to consider such things at that moment; I did not want to wonder 20 whether I was abandoning any hope of being with Erica. All I knew was that my days of focusing on fundamentals were done. And so, the following evening, two weeks ahead of schedule, I boarded a flight bound for New York.

Ah, our waiter approaches with green tea, the perfect aid to 25 digestion after a heavy meal. Remarkable service, eh? He has arrived just as he was required. One would not have thought, sir, that he was watching us so closely, but the night is now well advanced, and there are no longer any other customers to divert his attention.

3 **ensue** (fml): happen as a result of sth.   12 **propose** (fml): intend to do sth.
13 **replacement**: *Ersatzperson*   14 **up to speed**: having the most recent and
accurate information or knowledge about sth.   16 **impudent** ['ɪmpjʊdənt] (fml):
not showing respect for other people   18 **expire**: be no longer valid   19 **resolve to
do sth.**: make a firm decision to do sth.   26 **digestion**: *Verdauung*   29 **divert sth.**:
take sth. (e.g. sb.'s attention) away

11

It is odd how the character of a public space changes when it is empty; the abandoned amusement park, the shuttered opera house, the vacant hotel: in films these often feature as backdrops for events intended to frighten. So it is with this market: now that our fellow
5 visitors have dwindled in number to a sporadic and scattered few, it has taken on a rather more ominous edge. Perhaps it has to do with the cloudy sky above, through which one occasionally glimpses a gash of moon, or perhaps it is the darkening shadows in the warren of alleyways slipping away from here in all directions, but I would
10 suggest that it is instead our *solitude* that most disturbs us, the fact that we are all but alone despite being in the heart of a city. Ah! There, sir, do you smell it: the aroma of dust on that warm breeze? That is the smell of the desert to the south, a smell that, were we to encounter it in your homeland, would in all likelihood foreshadow
15 the passage through this dimly lit stage of a desolate ball of tumbleweed.

Although the atmosphere that surrounded me on my flight from Santiago to New York was precisely the opposite – the cabin was bright and close to full – my thoughts belonged to a setting like that
20 which you and I occupy at this moment. Yes, my musings were bleak indeed. I reflected that I had always resented the manner in which America conducted itself in the world; your country's constant interference in the affairs of others was insufferable. Vietnam, Korea,

---

2 **shuttered**: with the shutters (= *Fensterladen*) closed   3 **vacant**: empty, not being used   **backdrop**: background   5 **dwindle**: become gradually less or smaller
6 **ominous** ['ɑːmɪnəs]: suggesting that sth. bad is going to happen in the future
8 **warren**: passages like a rabbit's system of underground tunnels   10 **solitude**: the state of being alone   14 **foreshadow sth.** (fml): be a sign of sth. that will happen in the future   15 **passage** (fml): act of passing through   16 **tumbleweed**: type of plant that grows in semi-desert areas of America and is blown around like a ball by the wind   21 **bleak**: not giving any reason to have hope   22 **conduct yourself** (fml): behave in a particular way   23 **insufferable**: extremely unpleasant

the straits of Taiwan, the Middle East, and now Afghanistan: in each
of the major conflicts and standoffs that ringed my mother continent
of Asia, America played a central role. Moreover I knew from my
experience as a Pakistani – of alternating periods of American aid
and sanctions – that finance was a primary means by which the   5
American empire exercised its power. It was right for me to refuse to
participate any longer in facilitating this project of domination; the
only surprise was that I had required so much time to arrive at my
decision.

I resolved to look about me with an ex-janissary's gaze – with,   10
that is to say, the analytical eyes of a product of Princeton and
Underwood Samson, but unconstrained by the academic's and the
professional's various compulsions to focus primarily on parts, and
free therefore to consider also the *whole* of your society – upon my
return to New York. Seen in this fashion I was struck by how   15
traditional your empire appeared. Armed sentries manned the check
post at which I sought entry; being of a suspect race I was quarantined
and subjected to additional inspection; once admitted I hired a
charioteer who belonged to a serf class lacking the requisite
permissions to abide legally and forced therefore to accept work at 20
lower pay; I myself was a form of indentured servant whose right to
remain was dependent upon the continued benevolence of my
employer. *Thank you, Juan-Bautista,* I thought as I lay myself down in
my bed, *for helping me to push back the veil behind which all this had
been concealed!*   25

But I must have been in a peculiar emotional state, in a sort of
semi-hypnotic daze, for when I woke in the morning my feelings
were entirely different. It was then that I was hit by the enormity of
what I was giving up. Where else could I – without money and

---

2 **ring sth.**: happen in a circle around sth.   12 **unconstrained**: not restricted or
limited   13 **compulsion** (fml): strong pressure   16 **sentry**: a soldier whose job is
to guard sth.   **man sth.**: be in charge of sth. as part of your work   19 **charioteer**
[ˌtʃærɪəˈtɪr]: *Wagenlenker/in*   **serf** (old use): *Leibeigener/in*   20 **abide** (fml): stay or
live in a place   21 **indentured servant** (old use): servants or farmers contracted to
work for a fixed period of time in exchange for transportation, food, clothing, etc.
24 **veil**: *Schleier*   25 **conceal sb./sth.**: hide sb./sth.   27 **daze**: confused state of
mind

family contacts, and at so young an age – hope to attain such an impressive income? Would I not miss this city of possibility, with its magical vibrancy and sense of excitement? What about my duty to Erica, or rather the duty to myself that was born of my desire for
5   her? And how would I face Jim?

If you have ever, sir, been through the breakup of a romantic relationship that involved great love, you will perhaps understand what I experienced. There is in such situations usually a moment of passion during which the unthinkable is said; this is followed by a
10 sense of euphoria at finally being liberated; the world seems fresh, as if seen for the first time; then comes the inevitable period of doubt, the desperate and doomed backpedaling of regret; and only later, once emotions have receded, is one able to view with equanimity the journey through which one has passed. My doubt and regret came
15 rather quickly, as they so often – in my experience of our species – tend to do, and when I boarded the subway to report for duty at Underwood Samson for the last time, I was in a state of shock similar to that which one undergoes when one has witnessed one's knee twist impossibly but has yet to feel any pain.

20 Not – please understand me – that I was convinced that I had made a mistake; no, I was merely unconvinced that I had *not* made a mistake. I was, in other words, confused. Nevertheless, my pride compelled me to attempt to appear unaffected by the unexpected sadness within me. I did not permit my gaze to linger on the
25 imposing reception area – which struck me now as reminiscent of the gleaming façade of some exalted and exclusive temple – or on the spectacular view from our windows; I did not permit myself to pocket a box of my business cards, elegantly printed proof that I had once been selected from among hundreds to be here. I simply let
30 myself be led by the pair of security guards who stood on either side of me, watched as I placed a limited number of clearly personal

---

3 **vibrancy** [ˈvaɪbrənsi]: state of being full of life and excitement   11 **inevitable**: that you cannot avoid or prevent   12 **backpedal**: change an earlier opinion
23 **unaffected by sth.**: not changed or influenced by sth.   25 **imposing**: impressive

possessions into a small cardboard box, and then escorted me to human resources for my exit conversation.

This was surprisingly brief – stern and dauntingly formal, but without recrimination – and once the requisite forms had been signed and data relevant to performance-enhancing indicators gathered, I was told that Jim wanted to speak with me. He was wearing a dark suit and a dark tie – funereal colors, I thought – and he looked underslept. "You really screwed us, kid," he said. "I know," I replied. "I am sorry." "I'm not a big believer in compassion at the workplace," he went on. "I didn't think twice when it came to firing you. In fact, I wish I'd done it a month ago and saved us the headache you've given us down in Valparaiso. But," he paused, "I'll tell you this. I like you, Changez. I can see you're going through a crisis. If you ever need to get something off your chest and you want someone to talk to, call and I'll buy you a beer." My throat constricted; I could not reply. I nodded slowly, a gesture not unlike a bow.

After leaving Jim's office, I was marched to the elevator bank. I realized how deep was the suspicion I had engendered in my colleagues over these past few – bearded and resentful – weeks; only Wainwright came over to shake my hand and say farewell; the others, if they bothered to look at me at all, did so with evident unease and, in some cases, a fear which would not have been inappropriate had I been convicted of plotting to kill them rather than of abandoning my post in mid-assignment. The guards did not leave me until I was outside the building, and it was only then that I allowed myself to rub my eyes with the back of my hand, for they had been watering slightly.

---

2 **human resources**: *Personalabteilung*   3 **stern**: serious and disapproving
daunting (adj): making you feel nervous and less confident   4 **recrimination**:
accusation, esp. in response to a similar statement   **requisite** (fml): necessary for a
particular purpose   5 **enhancing**: improving the quality, value or status of sth.
8 **screw sb.** (sl): deal with sb. in a bad way   14 **get sth. off your chest** (infml): talk
about sth. that has been worrying you for a long time so that you feel less anxious
17 **elevator bank**: a row or series of elevators next to each other   18 **engender sth.**
(fml): create sth.   23 **convict sb. of sth.**: decide officially in court that sb. is guilty
of a crime   **plot sth.**: plan secretly to do sth. illegal

You must remember that I was only twenty-two and this had
been my first proper job; at such an age and in such a situation
events have an emotional resonance that is perhaps exaggerated. In
any case, I felt as though a world had ended – which, indeed, it had
5 – and I made my way to the East Village on foot. I imagine I was a
rather odd sight – a distraught and hirsute Pakistani carrying an
unmarked box through the center of Manhattan – but I do not recall
receiving any untoward comments from passersby; then again, I was
in all likelihood too preoccupied to have noticed.

10 In my flat I poured myself a whiskey and sat thinking. It was still
early – not yet midday – and so I decided to call my family. My
brother answered. He had received the money I had sent, he said,
and workers had already dug up and exposed our rotting pipes. By
tomorrow they ought to have been replaced. I told him that I had
15 decided to move back to Lahore. He attempted to dissuade me;
tension with India was mounting. He had been recently to Islamabad,
he said, and spouses and children of foreigners assigned to embassies
and NGOs were leaving the country. I explained that I had no choice;
"I got fired," I said, "and my visa will soon be invalid." He told me
20 the family would of course look after me. I did not say that I had
hoped to be the one looking after *them*, and I continued to cradle my
drink for some time after the call was done.

But your own glass, sir, has now remained empty a good while.
Shall I request our bill? A quick wave and yes, here he comes. How
25 much, you ask? Please do not worry yourself; you are a guest here
and this – it is only a tiny amount – is on me. You wish to pay half?
Absolutely not; besides, here we pay all or we pay none. You have
reminded me of how alien I found the concept of acquaintances
splitting a bill when I first arrived in your country. I had been raised

---

3 **resonance** (fml): strong reaction   6 **distraught** [dɪˈstrɑːt]: extremely upset and
anxious so that you cannot think clearly   **hirsute** [ˈhɜːsuːt]: having a lot of hair on
the face or body; (here) having a beard   15 **dissuade sb. from sth./doing sth.**:
persuade sb. not to do sth.   16 **mount**: increase gradually   18 **NGO = non-
governmental organization**: a charity, association, etc. that is independent of
government   21 **cradle sb./sth.**: hold sb./sth. gently   29 **split a bill**: share the
costs of sth. evenly

to favor mutual generosity over mathematical precision in such matters; given time both work equally well to even a score.

I had not, however, been schooled in the etiquette of how best to contact a lover who had retreated to a mental institution, and so I vacillated between emailing Erica and going to see her in person. In the end, my decision was made for me: I tried to email her but my message bounced back – with a notice saying it could not be delivered because her inbox was full – and so I rented a car and appeared at the facility unannounced. I was told at reception that visitors without invitations were not welcome – and in any case they could neither confirm nor deny if Erica was even there – but just as it seemed they were about to ask me to leave, I saw the nurse I had met on my previous trip and appealed to her to intervene on my behalf.

"I'll talk to him," she said to the receptionist, taking me aside. She looked flustered and suggested I sit down. "What do you know?" she asked me. "What do I know," I said, "about what?" "I'm so sorry," she said. "Erica's gone." I asked what precisely she meant, *gone*, and the nurse explained. Erica had vanished about two weeks ago, indeed shortly after I had seen her last. She had not liked to be alone when she had first come to the institution; she would spend hours with the nurses and the counselors and her fellow patients, and especially with the nurse with whom I was speaking. But towards the end of her stay she had increasingly been wandering off by herself, until one day she had walked out and not come back. Her clothes had been found on a rocky bluff overlooking the Hudson, neatly folded in a pile.

"Are you trying to tell me that she killed herself?" I said. "They haven't recovered any remains," the nurse said, "and she didn't leave a note. Technically she's a missing person. But she'd been saying goodbye to everyone." I asked if she could show me the place from which Erica might have jumped, and she led me through the

---

2 **even the score** (v): balance sth. out   5 **vacillate**: keep changing your opinion or thoughts about sth.   13 **intervene**: become involved in a situation in order to improve it   16 **flustered** (adj.): appearing nervous and/or confused   26 **bluff**: a steep cliff or slope, esp. by the sea or a river

grounds until we stood there. It was a beautiful spot to commit suicide, perhaps to run out from between the snow-dusted conifers, to push off from the granite and sail through the air, gazing across at the far bank of the mighty river, where a small house exhaled smoke
5 from its chimney, before crashing into the icy current below. But I could not imagine Erica's pale, naked body following that arc.

So I drove back to the city and went immediately to her apartment. Erica's mother was not wearing any makeup; I noticed her eyebrows were so fine as to be almost nonexistent. I explained
10 that I had just returned from the institution; had she heard from Erica? Her mother stared at me as though I had slapped her without provocation. "No," she said, recovering herself and speaking wearily, "I'm afraid not." "Please know," I said, "that I will do anything which is of assistance to you." "Thank you," she said, inviting me inside.
15 She told me that the emergency services would remain on the lookout for Erica, and ongoing advertisements had been purchased in the local newspapers; beyond that there was little one could do. We attempted to speak of inconsequential matters, but this proved difficult – when she asked how I was, I said I had just been fired;
20 when I asked the same, she could only muster a wan smile – and so we sat mainly in silence. But before I left, she did two things, I suspect out of kindness: first, she told me that Erica had mentioned that she had found me rather dashing in my new beard; and second, she gave me a copy of Erica's manuscript. "Maybe," her mother said,
25 "you'd like to read it."

I did not do so for over a week; it sat undisturbed on top of my television. During that time I waited for a sign from Erica – an email, a phone call, a ring on my buzzer – but none ever came. I wandered about the city revisiting places she had taken me to, whether because
30 I thought I might see her or because I thought I might see something of us, I am not now certain. A few of these places – such as the gallery in Chelsea we had visited on the night of our first date –

---

2 **conifer**: an evergreen tree with needles as leaves   12 **weary** ['wɪri]: tired
18 **inconsequential**: not important, trivial   20 **muster sth.** ['mʌstər]: *(hier) etwas
zustande bringen*   **wan** [wɑːn]: pale and weak   23 **dashing** (old-fashioned):
attractive, confident and elegant   28 **buzzer**: an electric doorbell

I proved unable to find; they had vanished as though they had never existed. Others, like the spot in Central Park where we had gone on our picnic, were easy to locate but seemed to have altered. Perhaps this was the effect of a change in season; perhaps also it was in the city's nature to be inconstant.   5

I remembered Erica in September, at what was still the start of our relationship, just after the attacks on the World Trade Center. Although it is traditionally associated with the end of summer and the impending arrival of autumn, September has always seemed to me a month of beginnings, a *spring* of sorts – possibly because it   10
marks the commencement of the academic year. I was diving into my life in New York in September, full of optimism at what was to come. One evening I was walking with Erica through Union Square and we saw a firefly. "Look!" she said, amazed. "It's trying to compete with the buildings." Indeed it was: a tiny greenish glow visible up   15
close but overwhelmed by the city's luminance when viewed from even a modest distance. We watched as it crossed Fourteenth Street, headed south. Erica stood in front of me, her back to my chest, and I placed my arms around her, resting my palms on her belly. It felt an intimate gesture – like that of an expectant father with his pregnant   20
wife – and she leaned against me. I can still recall the movement of her muscles as she breathed. A taxi sped by and we lost sight of the firefly. "Do you think he made it?" she asked me. "I have no idea," I said, "but I hope so."

Such memories occupied my waking hours in those days after   25
her disappearance, and likely also permeated my dreams; they were in that period my only form of contact with her. But eventually I did read the manuscript her mother had given me. I must admit, I was frightened to do so – as though it might be the last time I would hear Erica's voice – and I was nervous about what that voice might say. Yet   30
her novel was no tortured, obviously autobiographical affair. It was simply a tale of adventure, of a girl on an island who learns to make

---

1 **vanish**: disappear suddenly   3 **alter**: change, become different   16 **luminance**: the amount of light given out by sth.   20 **expectant**: having a baby soon or becoming a father

do. The narrative shimmered with hope, and although it was for the most part rather spare, it paused often to delight in little details: in the texture of the skin of a piece of fallen fruit, for example, or in the swaying antennas of crayfish in a stream.

5   I could not locate Erica in the rhythms or sounds of what she had written; it seemed a mistake, offered me no clues. It was so purposeful, so resolute in being precisely what it was that I was baffled. I was also powerfully affected. When I put down the manuscript, it was not with the conviction that Erica was either alive
10   or dead. But I had begun to understand that she had chosen not to be part of my story; her own had proven too compelling, and she was – at that moment and in her own way – following it to its conclusion, passing through places I could not reach. I saw I had no option but to pursue my own preparations to leave.

15   I would like to claim that my final days in New York passed in a state of enlightened calm; nothing could be further from the truth. I was an incoherent and emotional madman, flying off into rages and sinking into depressions. Sometimes I would lie in bed, thinking in circles, asking the same questions about why and where Erica had
20   gone; sometimes I would find myself walking the streets, flaunting my beard as a provocation, craving conflict with anyone foolhardy enough to antagonize me. Affronts were everywhere; the rhetoric emerging from your country at that moment in history – not just from the government, but from the media and supposedly critical
25   journalists as well – provided a ready and constant fuel for my anger.

   It seemed to me then – and to be honest, sir, seems to me still – that America was engaged only in posturing. As a society, you were unwilling to reflect upon the shared pain that united you with those

---

1 **shimmer**: shine with a soft light that seems to move slightly   8 **baffled**: confused   11 **compelling** (adj): requiring your complete attention   14 **pursue sth.**: do sth. or try to achieve sth. over a period of time   17 **incoherent**: unable to express yourself clearly, often because of emotion   **fly off into rages**: become extremely angry   20 **flaunt sth.**: show sth. you are proud of to other people, in order to impress or annoy them   21 **crave sth.**: have a very strong desire for sth. **foolhardy**: *tollkühn*   22 **antagonize sb.**: do sth. to make sb. angry with you **affront**: a remark or an action that insults or offends sb./sth.   27 **posturing**: behavior that is not sincere but is intended to attract attention

who attacked you. You retreated into myths of your own difference, assumptions of your own superiority. And you acted out these beliefs on the stage of the world, so that the entire planet was rocked by the repercussions of your tantrums, not least my family, now facing war thousands of miles away. Such an America had to be stopped in the interests not only of the rest of humanity, but also in your own.   5

I resolved to do so, as best I could. But first I had to depart. I rode to JFK on a crisp, clear afternoon, an afternoon that reminded me of my trip to the institution and the view from that bluff above the Hudson. I thought of Erica removing her clothes and then, having   10 shed her past, walking through the forest until she met a kindly woman who took her in and fed her. I thought of how cold she would have been on that walk. And so I left my jacket on the curb as a sort of offering, as my last gesture before returning to Pakistan, a wish of warmth for Erica – not in the way one leaves flowers for the   15 dead, but rather as one twirls rupees above the living. Later, through the windows of the terminal, I saw that I had caused a security alert, and I shook my head in exasperation.

What exactly did I do to stop America, you ask? Have you really no idea, sir? You hesitate – never fear, I am not so rude as to forcibly   20 extract an answer. I will tell you what I did, although it was not much and I fear it may well fail to meet your expectations. But first let us leave this market; the shutters are coming down, and some unsavory characters are lurking about. Where are you staying? The Pearl Continental, you say? I will walk you. No, it is not far, and   25 although it is dark and parts of our route will at this time be deserted, we should be fine. Lahore is, as I have said before, quite safe from the standpoint of petty crime – and besides we are both fortunately possessed of those aspects of stature and appearance that tend to give ruffians pause.   30

---

4 **repercussion**: *Auswirkung*   **tantrum**: sudden short period of angry, unreasonable childish behavior   8 **JFK**: a large international airport in New York, named after President John F Kennedy   13 **curb**: *Randstein*   17 **alert** (n): alarm
18 **exasperation**: the state of being annoyed by sb./sth. very much   24 **unsavory**: unpleasant   **lurk about**: hang around, usu. with illegal intentions   30 **ruffian**: a violent man, esp. one who commits crimes

12

From your backward glance, sir, I gather you have noticed that we
were not alone in our desire to depart. Yes, others have made their
way to Mall Road behind us, such as that waiter who was so
unusually attentive and yet seemed to rub against your grain. There
5 is nothing surprising in that; the evening's work is now done.
I would ask you to direct your gaze instead to these lovely buildings –
in varying states of disrepair – which date to the British era and
function geographically and architecturally as a link between the
ancient and contemporary parts of our city. How delightful they are:
10 a chemist, an optician, a purveyor of fine saris, a gentleman's tailor.
Observe how often the words *brothers* and *sons* appear in their
signage; these are family-run establishments, passed gently from
generation to generation. No, not in the case of that retailer of guns
and ammunition, as you correctly point out – but surely you must
15 concede for the most part that they are charming and rather quaint.

These plazas are a different matter entirely, with their harsh
outlines and cramped façades; they were built largely in the seventies
and eighties, before the instinct of historical preservation began to
take hold, and they mottle the surface of this area like an irritation of
20 the skin. I find them particularly unpleasant at night, unlit and
empty, bounded by those narrow passageways into which one could
imagine being dragged against one's will, forever to disappear! Yes,
you are quite right: let us quicken our pace; we have a fair distance
yet to cover.

---

4 **rub against sb's grain**: (here) irritate sb.   7 **disrepair**: the state of being in a bad
condition due to neglect or little care   **the British era**: the period from 1849 to
1947, when the British ruled over Lahore   10 **purveyor** (fml): *Händler/in*
13 **retailer**: *Einzelhändler/in*   17 **cramped**: without much space in between
façade [fə'sɑːd]: the front of a building   18 **preservation**: the act of keeping sth. in
its original state or in good condition   19 **mottle**: *sprenkeln, marmorieren*

Are you familiar with *The Legend of Sleepy Hollow?* You have seen
the film, you say? I have not, but I am sure it was faithful; certainly
the prose version was a most powerful work. One cannot but join in
the terror of poor Ichabod Crane, alone on his horse, in that moment
when he first perceives the presence of the Headless Horseman. 5
I must admit, I am sometimes reminded of the sound of those
spectral clip-clops when I go for nocturnal walks by myself. How
they make my heart pound! But clearly you do not share my pleasure
at this thought; indeed you appear decidedly anxious. Allow me,
then, to change the subject … 10

I had been telling you earlier, sir, of how I *left* America. The truth
of my experience complicates that seemingly simple assertion; I had
returned to Pakistan, but my inhabitation of your country had not
entirely ceased. I remained emotionally entwined with Erica, and I
brought something of her with me to Lahore – or perhaps it would 15
be more accurate to say that I lost something of myself to her that I
was unable to relocate in the city of my birth. Regardless, the effect
of this was to pull and tug at my moods; waves of mourning washed
over me, sadness and regret prompted at times by an external
stimulus, and at others by an internal cycle that was almost *tidal*, for 20
want of a better word. I responded to the gravity of an invisible
moon at my core, and I undertook journeys I had not expected to
take.

Often, for example, I would rise at dawn without having slept an
instant. During the preceding hours, Erica and I would have lived an 25
entire day together. We would have woken in my bedroom and
breakfasted with my parents; we would have dressed for work and

---

1 **The Legend of Sleepy Hollow**: a short story (1920) by American writer
Washington Irving about a Connecticut schoolmaster, Ichabod Crane, who
disappears on his ride home from a party, possibly the victim of a headless
horseman, who haunted the area   2 **faithful**: true to the original version
7 **spectral** (fml): like a ghost   **clip-clop**: the sound made by a horse's hoofs
nocturnal (fml): during the night   9 **decidedly**: definitely and in an obvious
way   14 **be entwined with sth.** [ɪn'twaɪnd]: be very closely involved or connected
with sth.   18 **pull and tug at sb.'s moods**: (here) cause sb. to change their feelings
often   20 **tidal** ['taɪdl]: connected with tides (= the regular rise and fall of the sea)

caressed in the shower; we would have sat on our scooter and driven
to campus, and I would have felt her helmet bumping against mine;
we would have parted in the faculty parking area, and I would have
been both amused and annoyed by the stares she received from the
5 students passing by, because I would not have known how much
those stares owed to her beauty and how much to her foreignness;
we would have gone out for an inexpensive but delicious dinner in
the open air, bathed by the moonlight beside the Royal Mosque; we
would have spoken about work, about whether we were ready for
10 children; I would have corrected her Urdu and she my course plan;
and we would have made love in our bed to the hum of the ceiling
fan.

I have also been transported in ways that were no less vivid but
far more fleeting. I recall once, during the monsoon, watching a
15 puddle form in the rut of a muddy tire track beside the road. As
raindrops fell and water filled the banks of this little lake, I noticed a
stone standing upright in the center, like an island, and I thought of
the joy Erica would have had at gazing upon that scene. Similarly, I
recall another incident, after I had a collision on my scooter, when I
20 returned home and stripped off my shirt to see a livid bruise on my
rib cage, where hers had once been. I stared at myself in the mirror
and touched my skin with my fingers and hoped that the mark
would not soon fade, as it inevitably did.

Such journeys have convinced me that it is not always possible to
25 restore one's boundaries after they have been blurred and made
permeable by a relationship: try as we might, we cannot reconstitute
ourselves as the autonomous beings we previously imagined
ourselves to be. Something of us is now outside, and something of
the outside is now within us. Perhaps you have had no comparable
30 experience, for you are gazing at me as though at a raving madman.
I do not mean to say that we are all *one*, and indeed – as will soon
become evident to you – I am not opposed to the building of walls

---

1 **caress**: touch sb./sth. gently, esp. in a sexual or loving way   3 **faculty**: all the
teachers of a particular university or college   15 **rut**: a deep track that a wheel
makes in soft ground   20 **livid**: dark bluish-grey in color   25 **blur sth.**: make sth.
less clear   26 **permeable**: *durchlässig*   30 **raving**: talking or behaving in a crazy
way

to shield oneself from harm; I merely wished to explain certain aspects of my behavior upon my return.

Despite my not insubstantial financial constraints, I managed every year to pay my class dues in order to receive the *Princeton Alumni Weekly,* which I read unfailingly from cover to cover, with 5 particular attention to the class notes and obituaries sections at the end. From time to time I would chance upon the name of an acquaintance and I would squint intently through such pinholes into the life I had left behind, wondering how that world – the world of people like those with whom I had traveled to Greece – was 10 evolving. Erica, however, never appeared in those pages, and while it was possible that mention of her had slipped by unnoticed in one of the issues that the vagaries of the international post had prevented from arriving, I drew hope and sorrow in equal measure from each of her episodic absences. 15

I do not know what I expected to find – a notice that her novel had been published and she had thrilled classmates by appearing at the book launch? a final announcement that her body had been identified? a blurry face in a reunion photograph that could plausibly have been hers? – but I do know that time did not diminish the 20 eagerness with which I looked. For some months I continued to email her, until her account became inactive; thereafter I limited myself to a single letter each year, sent on the anniversary of her disappearance, but it was always returned to me unopened.

My brother married last April, shortly before I turned twenty-five. 25 Subsequently my mother began to suggest – with increasing urgency – that I consider doing the same; she believed I was in the grip of an

---

1 **shield sb. from sth.**: protect sb./sth. from danger, harm or sth. unpleasant
3 **constraint**: a thing that limits or restricts sth. or your freedom to do sth.
4 **class dues** (pl): fees to be paid in order to retain privileges at the university you attended   4–5 **Princeton Alumni Weekly** [ə'lʌmnaɪ]: a magazine published for the alumni (= the former students) of Princeton University   6 **obituary** [ə'bɪtʃuəri]: a newspaper article about sb.'s life and achievements printed after their death
8 **squint**: look at sth. with your eyes partly shut in order to see better   13 **vagaries** (pl, fml): Launen   19 **reunion**: a social occasion attended by a group of people (e.g. who were at university together)   27 **in the grip of sth.**: experiencing sth. unpleasant that cannot be stopped

unhealthy melancholy and that a family of my own was the surest
way for me to rediscover satisfaction in my life. She also thought I
spent too much time at work or alone in my room, and not enough
with my friends. Once she even asked me with visible nervousness if
5   I was not, by any chance, gay. I had not told her about Erica, and I
found it became progressively more difficult to contemplate doing so;
our relationship could now thrive only in my head, and to discuss it
with a mother intent – admittedly in my own best interest – on
challenging it with reality might do it irreparable harm. Not, of
10 course, that I actually *believe* I am having a relationship, in the normal
sense of that term, with Erica at this moment, or that she will one day
appear, smiling and bent against the weight of her backpack, to
surprise me on my doorstep. But I am still young and see no need to
marry another, and for now I am content to wait.

15   You, sir, on the other hand, seem ready to bolt. What has so startled
you? Was it that sound in the distance? I assure you, it was not the
report of a pistol – although I can understand why you might think so
– but rather the misfiring exhaust of a passing rickshaw. Their two-
stroke motors, often not in the best of maintenance, are prone to
20 sputtering in that fashion. It is most disturbing, I agree. What? Is
somebody following us? I cannot see anyone – no, wait, now that you
mention it there are a few figures there, in the gloom. Well, we cannot
expect to have Mall Road to ourselves, even at this late hour. In all
likelihood they are merely workers making their way home.

25   Yes, you are right: they have paused. What do you mean, sir, did
I give them a signal? Of course not! I have as little insight into their
motivations and identities as you do. One can only speculate that
they have dropped something, or are engaged in conversation among
themselves. Or perhaps they are wondering why *we* have paused,

---

6 **progressively**: steadily and continuously   7 **thrive**: continue to be successful,
strong, healthy, etc.   8 **intent on doing sth.** (fml): determined to do sth.   15 **bolt**
(infml): run away in order to escape   **startle sb.**: surprise sb. suddenly in a way
that slightly shocks or frightens them   17 **report** (n): the sound of an explosion or
of a gun being fired   18 **exhaust**: *Auspuff*   **rickshaw**: a small light three-wheeled
vehicle used in some Asian countries to carry passengers   18–19 **two-stroke
motor**: *Zweitaktmotor*   19 **prone to sth.**: likely to suffer from sth. or to do sth. bad
20 **sputter**: make a series of short explosive sounds

and whether we mean them ill! Regardless, there is no need for us to concern ourselves overmuch; let us continue with our midnight stroll. Lahore is a city of eight million people, after all; it is hardly a rural forest inhabited by phantoms.

I am glad you are willing to proceed. But what are you searching 5 for? Ah, your unusual mobile phone. If you are sending a text to your colleagues, you may wish to inform them that we are not far from your hotel – another fifteen minutes at the most, I should think, which suggests to me that I ought to make haste if I am to bring matters to a suitable conclusion. Earlier, sir, if you recall, you 10 asked me what I did to stop America. Let me now, as we come to the end of our time together, attempt an answer, even though it may well leave you disappointed.

The threat of war with India reached its highest point the summer after I returned from New York. Multinational corporations on both 15 sides of the border ordered senior employees to leave, and travel advisories were issued throughout the nations of the First World, counseling their citizens to defer nonessential trips to our region. It seemed the weather was the only factor delaying the official commencement of hostilities: first because the heat was too great for 20 an Indian offensive in the desert, then because the monsoon's rains made driving treacherous for Indian tanks in the Punjab. September was deemed the best month for battle, since the mountain passes of Kashmir might be closed by snow as early as October. So we waited as our September ticked by – little noticed by the media in your 25 country, which was focused at that time on the first anniversary of the attacks on New York and Washington – and then the days started to shorten, the negotiations began to make progress, and the likelihood of a catastrophe that could have claimed tens of millions of lives receded. Of course, humanity's respite was brief: six months 30 later the invasion of Iraq would be under way.

---

1 **ill** (n, fml): harm   9 **make haste** (old-fashioned): hurry up   16–17 **travel advisory**: a warning not to travel to a certain place or country   18 **counsel sb.** (fml): advise sb.   **defer sth.** (fml): delay sth. until a later time   23 **deem sth. to be sth.**: consider sth. to be sth.   24 **Kashmir**: region occupied by India, Pakistan and China that has been a source of conflict between the three countries   29–30 **claim lives**: cause the death of people

A common strand appeared to unite these conflicts, and that was
the advancement of a small coterie's concept of American interests in
the guise of the fight against terrorism, which was defined to refer
only to the organized and politically motivated killing of civilians by
5 killers *not* wearing the uniforms of soldiers. I recognized that if this
was to be the single most important priority of our species, then the
lives of those of us who lived in lands in which such killers also lived
had no meaning except as collateral damage. This, I reasoned, was
why America felt justified in bringing so many deaths to Afghanistan
10 and Iraq, and why America felt justified in risking so many more
deaths by tacitly using India to pressure Pakistan.

I had in the meanwhile gotten a job as a university lecturer, and I
made it my mission on campus to advocate a disengagement from
your country by mine. I was popular among my students – perhaps
15 because I was young, or perhaps because they could see the practical
value of my ex-janissary's skills, which I imparted to them in my
courses on finance – and it was not difficult to persuade them of the
merits of participating in demonstrations for greater independence
in Pakistan's domestic and international affairs, demonstrations that
20 the foreign press would later, when our gatherings grew to
newsworthy size, come to label anti-American.

The first of our protests to receive much attention took place not
far from where we are now. Your country's ambassador was in town,
and we surrounded the building in which he was speaking, chanting
25 and holding placards. There were thousands of us, of all possible
affiliations – communists, capitalists, feminists, religious literalists –

---

1 **strand**: one of the different parts of an idea, a plan, a story, etc.   2 **advancement**:
the process of helping sth. to make progress or succeed   **coterie** ['kəʊtəri] (fml):
Seilschaft, Clique   3 **guise** [gaɪz]: a way in which sb./sth. appears, often in a way
that hides the truth about them/it   8 **collateral damage**: injury inflicted on sb./sth.
other than an intended target   11 **tacit**: *stillschweigend*   13 **advocate sth.** (fml):
support sth. publicly   **disengagement**: (here) the action of withdrawing
cooperation   16 **impart sth. to sb.**: pass on sth. (e.g. information) to sb.
18 **merit**: a good feature that deserves praise, reward or admiration   26 **affiliation**
(fml): a person's connection with a political party, religion, etc.   **religious literalist**:
a person who believes that a religious book like the Koran should be interpreted
literally

and things began to get out of hand. Effigies were burned and stones were thrown, and then we were charged at by large numbers of uniformed and plainclothed police. Scuffles broke out, I intervened in one, and as a result I spent the night in prison, nursing a bloody lip and bruised knuckles.   5

My office hours were soon overrun by meetings with politically minded youths, so much so that I was often forced to stay on until after dinner to ensure that I had dealt satisfactorily with the curricular and extracurricular demands of all those who sought me out. Naturally, I became a mentor to many of these men and women: 10 advising them not only on their papers and their rallies, but also on matters of the heart and a vast range of other topics – from drug rehabilitation and family planning to prisoners' rights and shelters for battered spouses.

I will not pretend to you that all of my students were angels; 15 some, I will be the first to admit, were no better than common thugs. But over the years I have developed the ability to take quick stock of a person – an ability that, I would be remiss not to point out, is in no small measure modeled on that of *my* former mentor, Jim – and while I will not claim to be infallible, I think it is fair to say that my 20 sense of another's character is generally very good. I can usually tell, for example, who in a crowd is most likely to provoke violence, or who among my peers is most likely to complain to the dean that I need to be put in my place before my activities get out of hand.

I have received official warnings on more than one occasion, but 25 such is the demand for my courses that I have until now escaped suspension. And lest you think that I am one of *those* instructors, in cahoots with young criminals who have no interest in education and

---

1 **effigy** ['efɪdʒi]: a model of a person that makes them look ugly   3 **scuffle**: a short and not very violent fight or struggle   14 **battered**: attacked violently and injured **spouse** (fml or law): a husband or wife   16 **common**: ordinary, not unusual or special   **thug**: a violent criminal person   17 **take stock of sb.**: judge sb. 18 **be remiss**: be negligent   20 **infallible**: never wrong   23 **dean**: a person in a university who is responsible for the discipline of students   27–28 **in cahoots with sb.** (infml): be planning or doing sth. dishonest with sb. else

who run their campus factions like marauding gangs, I should point out that the students I tend to attract are bright, idealistic scholars possessed of both civility and ambition. We call each other comrades – as, indeed, we do all those we consider like-minded –
5 but I would not hesitate to use the term *well-wishers* instead. So it was with immense consternation that I learned recently that one of them had been arrested for planning to assassinate a coordinator of your country's effort to deliver development assistance to our rural poor.

10   I had no inside knowledge of this supposed plot – which was all the more perverse for its alleged targeting of an agent of compassion – but I was certain that the boy in question had been implicated by mistake. How could I be certain, you ask, if I had no inside knowledge? I must say, sir, you have adopted a decidedly unfriendly
15 and accusatory tone. What precisely is it that you are trying to imply? I can assure you that I am a believer in nonviolence; the spilling of blood is abhorrent to me, save in self-defense. And how broadly do I define self-defense, you ask? Not broadly at all! I am no ally of killers; I am simply a university lecturer, nothing more nor
20 less.

I see from your expression that you do not believe me. No matter, I am confident of the truth of my words. In any case, it was impossible to ask the boy himself about the matter, as he had disappeared – whisked away to a secret detention facility, no doubt,
25 in some lawless limbo between your country and mine. He and I were not particularly well acquainted, as I have repeatedly testified, but I remembered his shy smile and aptitude for cash-flow statements, and I found myself filled with rage at the mystery

---

1 **faction**: small group of people who have the same objective   **marauding**: going around a place in search of things to steal or people to attack   3 **civility**: polite behavior   7 **assassinate sb.**: murder sb., esp. for political reasons   11 **alleged** [ə'ledʒd]: *mutmaßlich, angeblich*   15 **accusatory** [ə'kjuːzətɔːri] (fml): suggesting that you think sb. has done sth. wrong   17 **abhorrent** (fml): *zuwider, verabscheuungswürdig*   24 **detention facility**: place like a prison where people are kept in detention without trial   25 **limbo**: (here) a situation in which no real laws or rights apply   26 **testify**: make a statement that sth. happened or that sth. is true
27–28 **cash-flow statement**: *Kapitalflussrechnung*

surrounding his treatment. When the international television news
networks came to our campus, I stated to them among other things
that no country inflicts death so readily upon the inhabitants of
other countries, frightens so many people so far away, as America.
I was perhaps more forceful on this topic than I intended.   5

Later, it occurred to me that in addition to expressing my dismay,
I was possibly trying to attract attention to myself; I had, in my own
manner, issued a firefly's glow bright enough to transcend the
boundaries of continents and civilizations. If Erica was watching –
which rationally, I knew, she almost certainly was not – she might   10
have seen me and been moved to correspond. I was tugged at by an
undercurrent of loss when she did not do so. But my brief interview
appeared to resonate: it was replayed for days, and even now an
excerpt of it can be seen in the occasional war-on-terror montage.
Such was its impact that I was warned by my comrades that America   15
might react to my admittedly intemperate remarks by sending an
emissary to intimidate me or worse.

Since then, I have felt rather like a Kurtz waiting for his Marlow.
I have endeavored to live normally, as though nothing has changed,
but I have been plagued by paranoia, by an intermittent sense that I   20
am being observed. I even tried to vary my routines – the times I left
for work, for example, and the streets I took – but I have come to
realize that all this serves no purpose. I must meet my fate when it
confronts me, and in the meantime I must conduct myself without
panic.   25

Most of all, I must avoid doing what you are doing in this instant,
namely constantly looking over my shoulder. It seems to me that
you have ceased to listen to my chatter; perhaps you are convinced
that I am an inveterate liar, or perhaps you are under the impression

---

13 **resonate**: *Widerhall finden*   16 **intemperate** [ɪn'tempərət]: showing a lack of
control over yourself   17 **emissary** (fml): a person who is sent to deliver an official
message, esp. from one country to another, or to perform a special task   **intimidate
sb.**: frighten or threaten sb. so that they will do what you want   18 **Kurtz, Marlow**:
the two main characters from Joseph Conrad's novel *The Heart of Darkness* (1899),
with Marlow as the steamboat captain on a mission to take Kurtz out of the African
jungle and back to civilization   19 **endeavor** [ɪn'devər] : try very hard
29 **inveterate** [ɪn'vetərət] (fml): always doing sth. and unlikely to stop

that we are being pursued. Really, sir, you would do well to relax. Yes, those men are now rather close, and yes, the expression on the face of that one – what a coincidence; it is our waiter; he has offered me a nod of recognition – is rather grim. But they mean you no
5 harm, I assure you. It seems an obvious thing to say, but you should not imagine that we Pakistanis are all potential terrorists, just as we should not imagine that you Americans are all undercover assassins.

    Ah, we are about to arrive at the gate, of your hotel. It is here that you and I shall at last part company. Perhaps our waiter wants to say
10 goodbye as well, for he is rapidly closing in. Yes, he is waving at me to detain you. I know you have found some of my views offensive; I hope you will not resist my attempt to shake you by the hand. But why are you reaching into your jacket, sir? I detect a glint of metal. Given that you and I are now bound by a certain shared intimacy, I trust it is from the holder of your business cards.

---

7 **assassin**: a person who murders sb. for money or for political reasons   10 **detain sb.** (fml): delay sb. or prevent them from going somewhere   13 **glint**: a sudden flash of light or colour shining from a bright surface

Additional Texts

1
Book Review: The Hindustan Times

Pakistani author Mohsin Hamid's *The Reluctant Fundamentalist* is an incisive portrait of the transformation of a Princeton-educated Pakistani youth with a cushy American job and an American girlfriend into an America-baiting radical with a sneaking sympathy
5 for the 9/11 attackers.

In many ways, Hamid's novel dramatises simultaneous schizophrenia and romance with the American dream many educated Muslim youths experience as they go about making existential choices in a world caught in the treacherous currents of
10 East-West encounters.

The narrative is cunningly constructed as a monologue of Changez, a Pakistani 20-something young man who lands a plum job in New York and falls in love with the beautiful but troubled Erica (a subtle play on Am-Erica), with an unidentified American as
15 his sole listener in a restaurant in the famous old Anarkali Bazar in Lahore

This is, however, just the frame. Hamid's second novel after *Moth Smoke* (2000) has a more ambitious and apt theme as it digs deeper into the psychology of fundamentalism and the roots of Muslim
20 anger against an arrogant and insufferable America as it interferes in the affairs of others, be it "Vietnam, the Middle East and now Afghanistan", without being shrill or loud.

The bright and beautiful American dream turns sour for Changez one fine day in Manila where he had gone to value an ailing company

---

2 **incisive** [ɪnˈsaɪsɪv]: sharp, insightful   3 **cushy** (infml): very pleasant
4 **America-baiting**: deliberately making cruel or insulting remarks about America
sneaking: *verstohlen, heimlich*   9 **treacherous**: dangerous, esp. when seeming safe
current: *Strömung*   11 **cunning**: clever and skilful   12 **plum** (adj): considered very
good and worth having   15 **sole**: only   18 **apt**: suitable   20 **interfere in sth.**: *sich
in etwas einmischen*   24 **ailing**: having problems and getting weaker

for Underwood Samson, an elite firm that proudly flaunts "Focus on   25
the fundamentals" as its motto – an ironic reference to capitalist
fundamentalism as opposed to the one of Islamic variety.

As he switches on TV on that scary day in contemporary world
history – September 11, 2001 – he found his inner voice articulating
cultural conflicts he had chosen to gloss over in the midst of the   30
good things of life Manhattan offered.

"Yes, despicable as it may sound, my initial reaction was to be
remarkably pleased," observes Changez. This was his moment of
conversion; and from this point onwards his self-deprecating voice,
alternatively wry and witty, acquires an edge of touchiness and   35
anguish.

Another hinge moment in Changez's life occurs in Valparaiso
where he had gone to evaluate an old publishing company targeted
for a takeover.

Over lunch, the publisher, in an oblique hint at his predicament,   40
tells him the story of Janissaries of the Ottoman empire, who were
captured Christian boys trained to fight against their own people,
which they willingly did with singular ferocity.

"I was a modern-day Janissary, a servant of the American empire
at a time when it was invading a country with a kinship to mine …"   45
observes Changez in a biting moment of self-knowledge.

Hamid's novel is thus part fiction, part history and part polemics
that is firmly grounded in bruising realities of the post 9/11 world
and its troubled dialectic between Islam and the West.

It also illuminates the temptations of radicalism and   50
fundamentalism for well-heeled, educated youth who for all their
success in the West still feel a sense of deep alienation and ennui in

---

25 **flaunt sth.**: show sth. you are proud of to other people in order to impress them
30 **gloss over**: avoid talking about sth. unpleasant or embarrassing by not dealing
with it in detail   34 **conversion**: *Sinneswandel, Wandlung*   **self-deprecating**: done
in a way that makes your own achievements or abilities seem unimportant   35 **wry**:
ironic   37 **hinge moment**: key moment   40 **oblique**: indirect   **predicament**:
dilemma   43 **singular**: very great   **ferocity**: violence; aggressive behavior
47 **polemics** (pl, fml): the action of arguing strongly for or against sb./sth.
48 **bruising**: difficult and unpleasant   51 **well-heeled**: rich, wealthy   52 **ennui**:
the feeling of being bored and not satisfied because nothing interesting is happening

their adopted homelands, as was the case with the key perpetrators
of 9/11 attacks and more recently of some suspects in the failed UK
55 terror plot.

Not that they have a morally superior alternative in place.

Towards the end of the novel, the narrator, who has reluctantly
returned home, mocks at his own paranoia and that of his American
interlocutor. "It seems an obvious thing to say but you should not
60 imagine that we Pakistanis are all potential terrorists, just as we
should not imagine that you Americans are all undercover assassins."

It is in these troubled and self-conscious soliloquies one can find
insights into the misguided clash of civilisations that is being enacted
by fanatics on both sides of the divide.

From: Manish Chand, the Hindustan Times, *17 July 2007*

---

53 **perpetrator**: a person who commits a crime   58 **mock (at) sth.**: make fun of
sth.

2

Book Review: The New York Times

This is a book that pivots on a smile. A third of the way through Mohsin Hamid's second novel, *The Reluctant Fundamentalist*, the narrator, a young Pakistani man named Changez, tells an American how he first learned of the destruction of the World Trade Center. While on a business trip to Manila, he turned on the television in his 5 hotel room and saw the towers fall. "I stared as one – and then the other – of the twin towers of New York's World Trade Center collapsed. And then I smiled. Yes, despicable as it may sound, my initial reaction was to be remarkably pleased."

The novel begins a few years after 9/11. Changez happens upon 10 the American in Lahore, invites him to tea and tells him the story of his life in the months just before and after the attacks. That monologue is the substance of Hamid's elegant and chilling little novel.

In 2001, as he explains, Changez was hardly a radical. Fresh out 15 of Princeton, he was living in New York City and working as a financial analyst. He appears to have been something of a cipher, until his reaction to the attacks – that sudden smile – pierces the shell. It seems to have come as a surprise even to himself, and while hardly endearing, it sets his tale in motion. 20

A less sophisticated author might have told a one-note story in which an immigrant's experiences of discrimination and ignorance cause his alienation. But Hamid's novel, while it contains a few such moments, is distinguished by its portrayal of Changez's class aspirations and inner struggle. His resentment is at least in part self- 25 loathing, directed at the American he'd been on his way to becoming.

---

1 **pivot on sth.**: be centred on sth.   10 **happen upon sb./sth.**: find sb./sth. by chance   13 **chilling** (adj): frightening   17 **cipher** ['saɪfər] (infml): a person without a strong character   18 **pierce sth.**: break through sth.   19 **shell**: *Schale* 25 **resentment**: *Verbitterung, Groll*   25–26 **self-loathing**: hating yourself

For to be an American, he declares, is to view the world in a certain way – a perspective he absorbed in his eagerness to join the country's elite.

30   His indoctrination, however, was never total. Starting with his job interview at Underwood Samson, a small firm that appraises businesses around the world, and a postgraduation trip to Greece with friends from Princeton, Changez maintains an outsider's double perspective. On the trip he is smitten with Erica, one of the other
35   travelers, but is also bothered by his rich friends' profligate spending and the condescension with which they give orders to anyone they've paid for a service: "I ... found myself wondering by what quirk of human history my companions – many of whom I would have regarded as upstarts in my own country, so devoid of refinement
40   were they – were in a position to conduct themselves in the world as though they were its ruling class." Yet even as he recognizes the foibles of that ruling class, Changez, who comes from a high-status but downwardly mobile family, also aspires to join it. Given his oft-mentioned phenomenal aptitude for his new job and a talent for
45   winning over other people, that goal seems all but guaranteed.

By the time he reaches Manila, where he is sent to appraise a recording business, Changez finds himself trying to assert his Americanness. Suddenly he's the one ordering around men his father's age. Unnerved when a jeepney driver gives him a hostile
50   look, Changez puzzles over its significance until he glances at one of his colleagues and feels his own hostility toward the other man's "oblivious immersion" in his work.

So which is he, the ignorant master or the canny subaltern? And has he sacrificed his identity in pursuit of status? Changez has
55   already begun to ask himself these questions when he sees the towers fall. And in the wake of the attacks, as tensions escalate between India and Pakistan, and the United States is meanwhile

---

28 **eagerness**: *Eifer*   31 **appraise sth.**: decide who much sth. is worth   34 **be smitten with sb.**: have strong feelings for sb.   35 **profligate** ['prɑ:flɪgət]: spending money in a careless way   42 **foible**: strange or weak aspect of a person's character   47 **assert sth.**: push sth. forward   53 **subaltern**: person who is subordinate to another

caught up in patriotic displays that strike Changez as a dangerous form of nostalgia, he loses interest in his work. Assigned to help appraise a publishing company in Valparaiso, Chile, he spends his time visiting Neruda's house and lunching with the publisher, who compares Changez to a janissary – one of the Christian youths captured and then conscripted by the Ottomans, compelled to do battle against their own civilization.

Yet there is still the matter of his beloved Erica, who is friendly with Changez but mourning the death of her former boyfriend, Chris, from lung cancer. Changez is polite and formal; Erica is uninhibited, going topless, for instance, on a beach in Greece. The two become intimate, but she is haunted by Chris, and after 9/11 her sadness mysteriously turns pathological. She lands in an institution, then disappears.

This part of the story seems a bit too convenient – Erica's obsession with the past engineered to dovetail with America's nostalgia and with Changez's yearning for a lost Lahore – while her disappearance neatly parallels his departure from America. (Our hero's name gets no points for subtlety either.) Hamid, who himself attended Princeton and worked in corporate America, aptly captures the ethos and hypocrisies of the Ivy League meritocracy, but less so its individual members. Throughout the book, secondary characters are sketched rather than distinctively rendered.

We never learn the American man's identity, yet Changez regularly interrupts the story to address him. Perhaps, it is suggested, he had been pursuing Changez, who has become a leader of anti-American protests. Apparently, the man is "on a mission" – and he may be carrying a weapon. While these interruptions come too frequently for my taste, they do lend his tale an Arabian Nights-style urgency: the end of the story may mean the death of the teller.

It seems that Hamid would have us understand the novel's title ironically. We are prodded to question whether every critic of

---

68 **uninhibited**: behaving freely without worrying about what other people might think   73 **dovetail with sth.**: fit in very well with sth.   74 **yearning** (n): *Sehnsucht*   77 **apt**: *geschickt*   80 **render sb.**: (here) develop sb., create sb.
89 **prod sb.**: push sb.

90   America in a Muslim country should be labeled a fundamentalist, or whether the term more accurately describes the capitalists of the American upper class. Yet these queries seem blunter and less interesting than the novel itself, in which the fundamentalist, and potential assassin, may be sitting on either side of the table.

From: Karen Olsson, The New York Times, *22 April 2007*

3
My Reluctant Fundamentalist

In this text, the author of The Reluctant Fundamentalist, *Mohsin Hamid, examines the background to the writing of the novel.*

In the summer of 2000, I began writing my second novel. I was living on Cornelia Street in New York's West Village, working as a management consultant at McKinsey & Company with the unusual understanding that I would be allowed to disappear from the office for three months a year to write. I was close to paying off the hundred   5
thousand dollars of loans I had taken out to finance law school; I had published my first novel, *Moth Smoke,* a few months earlier; and I was able to return regularly for extended periods to Lahore, the city in Pakistan where I had mostly grown up. The time had come for me to decide what to do with my life, and where to do it.   10

The choices I faced were confusing. New York or Lahore? Novelist as my entire profession or as only a part? And the choices were related. If I left my job to write full time, I would lose my employment-based work visa and be forced to depart permanently for Pakistan. As I had done once before, I turned to my writing to   15
help me understand my split self and my split world. *Moth Smoke* had for me been a look at Pakistan with a gaze altered by the many years I had spent in America. *The Reluctant Fundamentalist,* I thought, would be a look at America with a gaze reflecting the part of myself that remained stubbornly Pakistani.   20

By the summer of 2001 I had produced a draft. I had consciously moved away from the multiple first-person narration and freestyle riffs of *Moth Smoke.* I had instead written a stripped-down, utterly

3 **consultant**: an expert that provides help and assistance   6 **loan**: money that a person borrows   14 **employment-based**: given on the condition that sb. has got a job   17 **gaze**: way of looking   **alter sth.**: change sth.   20 **stubborn**: determined not to change your opinion or attitude   23 **riff**: (usu. in music) a short repeated phrase   **stripped-down**: keeping only the essential features

minimalist love story of a young Pakistani man in New York who is
25 troubled by the notion that he is a modern-day janissary serving the
empire of American corporatism. The style was that of a fable, of a
parable, the kind of folk or religious story one looks to for guidance,
because of course guidance was what I needed.

But upon reading it my agent told me he was puzzled by the
30 protagonist's inner conflict: why would so secular and westernized a
Muslim man feel such tension with America? I told him there was
deep resentment in much of the rest of the world towards the sole
remaining superpower, and I resigned myself to a process of writing
that would mirror that of my first novel, which took some seven
35 drafts and seven years to complete. I also accepted a temporary
transfer to my firm's London office as a way of deferring my life
decisions, thinking the city lay geographically and culturally midway
between New York and Lahore. I left America shortly after my
thirtieth birthday in July, and so it was from across the Atlantic in
40 September that I watched the World Trade Center fall in a place I
still thought of as home.

The rest of that year was one of great turmoil for me. Muslim
friends of mine in America began to be questioned and harassed;
I was upset by the war in Afghanistan; traveling on my Pakistani
45 passport became increasingly unpleasant; and then, following the
December terrorist attacks on India's parliament, it looked as though
India might invade Pakistan. Lahore sits on the border, just a few
miles from what would have been the front line. I knew I needed to
be there with my family. So I took a leave of absence and went back,
50 moving into my old room.

That crisis eventually passed. But my novel made little progress.
I had chosen to keep it set in the year before September 11, so that
my characters would not be overwhelmed by an event that spoke so
much more loudly than any individual's story could. I grew personally
55 more divided, saddened and angered by the heavy-handedness of the

25 **notion**: idea or belief   27 **guidance**: direction, help   30 **secular**: worldly, not
religious   32 **resentment**: bitterness, anger   **sole**: only   36 **defer sth.**: delay sth.
until a later time   42 **turmoil**: chaos, disorder   43 **harass sb.**: *jdn. belästigen*
55 **heavy-handedness**: the inability of showing a sympathetic understanding of the
feelings of other people

Bush administration's conduct abroad. I decided to make my transfer
to London permanent. I then met the woman I would later marry
while she was visiting the city on a holiday and was inspired to quit
my job. Until she moved to London after our wedding, I was often on
airplanes between there and Lahore.   60

Eventually, I realized that, just as in my exterior world, there was
no escaping the effects of September 11 in the interior world that
was my novel. The story of a Pakistani man in New York who leaves
just before that cataclysmic event would inevitably be bathed in the
glare of the reader's knowledge of what would happen immediately   65
after. I also felt enough time had passed for me to have something of
the distance that distinguishes a novelist's perspective from a
journalist's. So I re-wrote the novel once again, this time set around
the period of September 11, and I finished early in 2005.

The novel was still short, and the basic arc of the plot was   70
unchanged. But I had chosen to shift the voice into an American-
accented first person. My intention was to tell a story that felt, for
the first one third, deceptively familiar, a tale of the sort of American
dream now so often told that it lulls us into a lazy complacency.
Then, relying on the strength of that bond between reader and   75
narrator, I would venture into more and more emotionally disturbing
territory.

This did not entirely work, unfortunately, as my agent and former
editor made clear to me when they read it. But I could see I was close
to something now. For me, writing a novel is like solving a puzzle.   80
I had tried variations of minimalism in the third person, with voices
ranging from fable to noir. I had tried the comforting oral cadences
of an American accented first person. But there was not enough of
Pakistan in my novel, and it felt wrong somehow both to my ear, in
its sound, and to my eye, in its architecture.   85

---

56 **conduct** (fml): behavior   64 **cataclysmic**: catastrophic   70 **arc**: *Handlungsbogen*
73 **deceptive**: misleading   74 **complacency** [kəm'pleɪsənsi]: *Selbstzufriedenheit*
76 **venture**: go somewhere which may be dangerous or unpleasant   82 **(film) noir**:
a style of making movies in which there are strong feelings of fear or evil   **cadence**
['keɪdəns] (fml): *Tonfall*

But I was energized by this near miss, and I soon had my answers: the frame of a dramatic monologue in which the Pakistani protagonist speaks to an American listener, and a voice born of the British colonial inflections taught in elite Pakistani schools and colored by
90   an anachronistic, courtly menace that resonates well with popular western preconceptions of Islam. Even as I wrote it I knew it would be the final draft. I was done a year later, in February 2006, and it sold almost immediately.

Writing now, in March 2007, as *The Reluctant Fundamentalist* is
95   finally born, I feel its difficult gestation has helped me. I am still split between America and Pakistan. But I feel more comfortable with my relationship to both places than I have in a long time. People often ask me if I am the book's Pakistani protagonist. I wonder why they never ask if I am his American listener. After all, a novel can often be
100   a divided man's conversation with himself.

From: Mohsin Hamid, website of Powell's books

86 **near miss**: thing that nearly hits what it is aimed at but misses it   89 **inflection**: a change in how high or low your voice is as you are speaking   90 **anachronistic**: outdated, old-fashioned   **courtly**: polite   **menace** threat   **resonate**: find acceptance   91 **preconception**: an idea or opinion that is formed before you have enough information   95 **gestation** [dʒeˈsteɪʃən]: (here) process of creation

4
Pakistan and Lahore

The information below is from Lonely Planet, the largest travel guide publisher in the world.

Introducing Pakistan

Pakistan has been on the brink of being tourism's "next big thing" for more years than we care to remember. It's a destination that has so much to offer visitors; drive the Karakoram Highway through the endless peaks of the Karakoram Mountains, or wander through the architectural glories of the former Mughal capital Lahore, the ancient 5 bazaars of Quetta or the cosmopolitan streets of Karachi. But every time the country seems to be gearing up to refresh the palates of travellers jaded with last year's hip destination, world media headlines send things off the rails – again. No matter the attractions, tourism in Pakistan has always been something of a hard sell. A 10 glance at the map shows the country living in a pretty difficult region: always-unruly Afghanistan to one side, Iran to another, and a border with India running through the 60-year-old fault line of Kashmir. But since the events of 9/11, Western pundits have increasingly been wondering if Pakistan isn't just living in a tough 15 neighbourhood, it is the tough neighbourhood.

Pakistan and political stability have never been particularly happy bedfellows. President Pervez Musharraf, who seized power in a 1999 coup, looked to have an unassailable position until relatively recently. Selling himself as a bulwark against radical Islamism on one 20

---

1 **be on the brink of sth.**: be very close to sth. that is new, exciting, or dangerous
7 **gear up for sth.**: prepare yourself for sth.   **palate** ['pælət]: Gaumen   8 **jaded**:
tired and bored, usu. because you have seen or had too much of sth.   9 **send sth.
off the rails**: *etwas aus den Fugen geraten lassen*   12 **unruly**: disobedient,
uncontrollable   14 **pundit**: expert   19 **unassailable** (fml): that cannot be defeated
20 **bulwark** ['bʊlwək] (fml): barricade

hand and the old corrupt elites on the other, he turned himself into a key player in Washington's 'War on Terror' and was rewarded with soft loans and military aid. In 2007, everything was thrown into disorder. An attempt to sack the country's chief justice resulted in a
25 red-faced retreat in the face of middle-class protests. At the same time, domestic Islamists stepped up their bloody campaigns in the wake of the deadly storming of Islamabad's Red Mosque. Pakistan's army had already found itself fighting to a standstill in the lawless Tribal Areas along the Afghan border, and later quelling related
30 violence in the Swat Valley. It signed the short-lived Waziristan Compact that negotiated a peace – of sorts – with Pakistani Taliban, but ultimately showed that having once given official government sanction to such radicals, it was now holding a tiger by its tail.

It was anyone's guess how Musharraf's attempts to pull things
35 together would play. The imposition of a state of emergency curtailed the press and judiciary, and soon after being lifted, the country was rocked by the assassination of Benazir Bhutto, recently returned from exile to take her place again in Pakistani politics. Such a high profile murder presaged a potentially very troubled future for
40 Pakistan. But against this background, there is another Pakistan, a world away from the headlines. Although conservative, Pakistanis are by nature a welcoming and hospitable people to foreigners, trying to get by in the face of indifference from their government and occasional hostility from the outside world. High politics is of less
45 interest than jobs and the cost of cooking oil and flour. As such, travellers are usually met with genuine interest and enthusiasm. The scams and hustle you might experience in heavily travelled India are nowhere to be seen here. Instead, look forward to spontaneously offered cups of tea and conversations about cricket. You'll feel like

---

24 **sack sb.** (infml): fire sb.   25 **red-faced**: showing embarrassment   26 **step up sth.**: increase sth.   26–27 **in the wake of sth.**: coming after or following sth.
29 **quell sth.** (fml): attempt to stop sth. (e.g. violent behavior or protests)
35 **imposition**: the act of introducing sth. (e.g. a new law or rule)   **curtail sth.** [kɔr'teɪl] (fml): *etwas einschränken*   39 **presage sth.** (fml): be a warning or sign that sth. unpleasant will happen   43 **indifference**: lack of interest or sympathy
46 **genuine**: real   47 **scam**: *Gaunerei*

you have the country to yourself. Attractions that would have been 50
splashed over the glossy pages of newspaper travel supplements are
almost empty. While enthusiastic travel advice comes tinged with
official government travel advisories, you'll need to keep one eye on
the news before booking your ticket – but once here, you'll realise
that Pakistan really is one of the world's best-kept travel secrets. 55

Introducing Lahore

Although Lahore may not be Pakistan's capital city, it wins hands
down as its cultural, intellectual and artistic hub. If history and
architecture are your passion there's an evocative mix, from
formidable Mughal monuments to faded legacies of the British Raj.
Indeed, even a ramble around the Old City can unfold into a mini- 60
adventure. For those in search of spiritual sustenance, Lahore has
qawwali (Islamic devotional singing) and Sufism (Islamic mysticism)
that will blow your mind.

Pakistan is crazy about cricket and one way of breaking the ice
with Lahorites is to strike up a conversation about the game. 65
Lahore – which, incidentally, is home to former cricket great turned
politician Imran Khan – sometimes serves as the venue for high-
profile international matches. If there's one on during your stay it's
worth experiencing it as much for its wildly ecstatic spectators as for
the game itself. 70

Over the years Lahore has burgeoned into a bustling and
increasingly polluted metropolis with festering social undercurrents,
but it also has some of the most defiantly serene architecture and
gardens on the subcontinent. It takes more than just a couple of days
to get to know this splendid city, so don't regard it merely as a 75

51 **splash sth. over sth.**: put sth. (e.g. a photograph) in sth. (e.g. the front page of a
newspaper) where it will be easily noticed   **supplement**: an extra separate section,
often in the form of a magazine, that is sold with a newspaper   52 **tinge sth. with
sth.**: add sth. (e.g. a particular emotion) to sth.   56–57 **win hands down** (infml):
be easily the winner of a contest   57 **hub**: hotspot, centre   59 **legacy**:what is left
from the past   60 **ramble**: walk   61 **sustenance** (fml): food   71 **burgeon** (fml):
begin to grow or develop rapidly   72 **festering**: *zunehmend sich verschärfend*
73 **serene**: calm and peaceful

jumping-off point to nearby India. And whatever you do, make absolutely sure your stay in Lahore includes an afternoon on the outskirts in Wagah and at least one Thursday.

Dangers & annoyances

Most travellers have nothing but praise for Lahorites. Indeed, it's
80 most likely that you'll receive many invitations to chat over a hot cuppa. Unfortunately there are some less honourable souls who view travellers as an easy way of earning a quick buck. To avoid a prickly predicament make a mental note of the following scams encountered by fellow travellers.
85   A handful of crooked cops continue to tarnish the reputation of Lahore's police force. Travellers have been approached, generally after dark, by policemen making all manner of allegations to intimidate them into paying a bribe. Stay cool, stand your ground, and insist that they take you to the Chief of City Police and contact
90 your embassy.

From: the website of Lonely Planet

---

83 **prickly**: difficult to deal with   **predicament**: dilemma, difficult situation
85 **crooked** ['krʊkɪd]: dishonest   **tarnish sth.**: spoil the good opinion people have
of sth.   87 **allegation**: *Anschuldigung*

5
Map of Pakistan

Legend:
- International Boundary
- Line of Control
- Administrative Boundary
- National Capital
- City or Town

TURKMENISTAN

TAJIKISTAN

CHINA

Kyber
Pakhunkhwa

Kabul

Peshawar

Kashmir

Islamabad

Rawalpindi

AFGHANISTAN

Federally
Administered
Tribal Areas

Indus

Lahore

Punjab

Ravi

Balochistan

New Delhi

Indus

IRAN

Sindh

INDIA

Hyderabad

Karachi

Arabian Sea

0   200   400   600 km

6
Why We're Stuck with Pakistan

This text examines the troubled relationship between the USA and Pakistan in recent years.

When the U.S. confronted Pakistan after the terrorist attacks of Sept. 11, 2001, there were no discussions of common goals and shared dreams. There was just a very direct threat: you're either with us or against us. Pakistan had to choose between making an enemy
5 of the U.S. and taking a quick and dirty deal sweetened with the promise of a lot of cash. In the end, Pakistan's cooperation was a transaction that satisfied the urgent needs of the day, brokered by a nervous military dictator, Pervez Musharraf, who failed to explain the value of the U.S. relationship to his people. That allowed a theme
10 to become fixed among Pakistanis: the war on terrorism was America's war. When Pakistani soldiers started dying in battles with militant groups, when suicide bombers began killing Pakistani civilians, it was America's fault because it was America's war.

So as Pakistanis processed the mission that killed Osama bin
15 Laden, many concluded that they had been betrayed by their supposed ally. How dare the Americans sneak into the country without so much as a warning and conduct a military operation just 75 miles (120 km) from the capital? But they felt betrayed too by their military. How could it be that Pakistan's armed forces, which
20 claim a lion's share of government spending, were clueless about the presence, a mere mile from the country's most prestigious defense academy, of the world's most wanted terrorist? Cyril Almeida, one of Pakistan's best-known opinion writers, summed up the national anguish in a column: "If we didn't know [bin Laden was in

7 **broker sth.**: arrange the details of sth. (e.g an agreement)   14 **process sth.**: deal with sth. (e.g. new information)   16 **sneak**: go somewhere secretly, trying to avoid being seen   17 **conduct sth.**: carry out sth.   24 **anguish** (n): severe pain, mental suffering or unhappiness

Abbottabad], we are a failed state; if we did know, we are a rogue   25
state."

Pakistan is a bit of both. It's not hard to detect dysfunction in a
state where the military controls foreign policy, national security and
an intelligence network so pervasive that no dinner guest at a foreign
journalist's house goes unscrutinized. The civilian government,   30
hobbled by incompetence and corruption, has no power and, even
worse, no backbone. In tea shops and on street corners, Pakistanis'
frustration with their leadership collides with their inability to
change it. Instead they lash out at the U.S. for reminding them of
their failure as a nation.   35

The consequence is what Pakistani Prime Minister Yousuf Raza
Gilani, in an interview with *Time*, calls a "trust deficit" with the U.S.
Gilani insists that he can't mend the relationship with a wave of his
hand. "I am not an army dictator. I'm a public figure," he tells *Time*.
"If public opinion is against [the U.S.], then I cannot resist it to stand   40
with you. I have to go with public opinion." In a May 9 speech to
Parliament on the Abbottabad raid, Gilani accused the U.S. of
violating Pakistan's sovereignty and warned that Pakistan had the
right to retaliate with "full force" against any future incursions.
Others are more blunt: "To hell with the Americans," says retired   45
Brigadier General Shaukat Qadir, a popular columnist and regular
guest on TV talk shows. "We need to reconsider our relationship."

In Washington, that sentiment is echoed in Congress, where
lawmakers are demanding to know why a country that has received
more than $20 billion in U.S. aid over the past decade shelters and   50
arms enemies of the U.S. even as it purports to hunt them down.
"I think this is a moment when we need to look each other in the eye

---

25 **failed state**: *gescheiterter Staat*   25–26 **rogue state**: *Schurkenstaat*
27 **dysfunction**: the situation in which relationships within a society, family, etc. are
not working normally   29 **pervasive**: felt everywhere   30 **unscrutinized**: without
being looked at or examined carefully   31 **hobble sth.**: slow sth. down   34 **lash
out at sb./sth.**: criticize sb./sth. in an angry way   38 **mend sth.**: repair sth.
44 **retaliate**: hit back, take action as a response to sth.   **incursion**: a sudden attack
on a place by foreign armies, etc.   45 **blunt**: very direct   51 **purport to do sth.**:
claim to do sth., when this may not be true

and decide, Are we real allies? Are we going to work together?" said Speaker of the House John Boehner.

55   It's not just the rhetoric that's heating up. Each side seems eager to poke the other in the eye. The U.S. has launched drone strikes at several sites in Pakistan since the Abbottabad operation, knowing full well that these will infuriate the Pakistani military, which sees them as a violation of sovereignty. For their part, Pakistani officials

60   have told ABC News that they may give China parts of a destroyed U.S. stealth helicopter left behind at bin Laden's compound.

Yet for all the anger in Islamabad and Washington, neither nation has much of a choice. However duplicitous and volatile it may be, the U.S.-Pakistan relationship is central to the interests of both

65   countries. The U.S. needs Pakistan's help to be successful in Afghanistan. Pakistan provides, among other things, a vital transit link for goods destined for coalition troops in the landlocked country. But even without Afghanistan, the U.S. would need Pakistan to be stable. The alternative – a collapsing nation awash with terrorist

70   groups and possessing a nuclear arsenal – is too awful to consider. […]

The relationship, in truth, has never been about trust. It was and is a strategic alliance founded on complementary interests: Pakistan's desire for military assistance and its fear of becoming a pariah state,

75   and the U.S.'s need for regional support in the Afghanistan war. While Pakistan and the U.S. share similar long-term goals – economic partnership, stability in the region – their short-term needs rarely intersect. That is why the question of whose side Pakistan is on is so galling to most Pakistanis and so infuriating to

80   most Americans. "Pakistan is on Pakistan's side," says Tariq Azim, an opposition Senator and Deputy Information Minister under Musharraf.

---

54 **Speaker of the House**: chief official in the US House of Representatives
56 **drone strike**: an attack with an aircraft without a pilot, controlled from the ground   58 **infuriate sb.**: make sb. very angry   61 **stealth helicopter**: *Tarnkappenhubschrauber*   63 **duplicitous** [duˈplɪsətəs] (fml) : dishonest   **volatile**: unstable, unpredictable   67 **landlocked**: having no access to the sea   69 **awash with sth.**: overflowing with sth.   74 **pariah state** [pəˈraɪə]: a state that is politically isolated due to unacceptable behavior   79 **galling** [ˈɡɑːlɪŋ]: annoying, infuriating

Carved from the newly independent India in 1947, Pakistan has never fully resolved the quandary with which its founder, Mohammed Ali Jinnah, wrestled: Is it a Muslim state or a state for   85 Muslims? While his Indian counterpart, Jawaharlal Nehru, ruled for nearly two decades – long enough to realize his vision of a secular state – Jinnah died a year after Pakistan's founding. A succession of weak civilian governments and military dictatorships followed. In that period, India and Pakistan fought three wars, mainly over the   90 contested territory of Kashmir. In 1971, Indian military support for separatists in East Pakistan led to the creation of Bangladesh. That humiliation informs Pakistan's actions still and its belief that India constitutes an "existential threat" capable of destabilizing and further dismembering Pakistan. That fear of India, in turn, explains   95 Islamabad's quest for nuclear weapons, which was realized with a test in 1998.

For the first three decades of Pakistan's existence, its leaders, both military and civilian, ran a largely secular state. That changed in 1977, when General Zia ul-Haq took power in a military coup. He   100 cemented his rule by instituting Islamic law and revising the educational curriculum in an effort to promote nationalism and an Islamic identity. Had it not been for the 1979 Soviet invasion of neighboring Afghanistan, Pakistan's secular elite might have rebelled. Instead the country rallied in support of its neighbor, out of fear that   105 it might be next.

Fearing the same thing, the U.S. supported Pakistan as it armed and trained Afghan mujahedin to take on the Soviets. This required both subterfuge and a certain amount of denial: since U.S. law forbade aid to a nation pursuing nuclear weapons, Washington   110

---

83 **carve sth.**: divide sth. into smaller parts   84 **quandary**: *Zwickmühle*
87–88 **secular state**: a state not influenced or governed by religion   91 **contested**: fought over   93 **humiliation**: the act of making sb. feel ashamed or stupid and lose the respect of other people   **inform sth.** (fml): have an influence on sth.
95 **dismember sth.** (fml): divide sth. (e.g. a country, an organization) into smaller parts   102 **curriculum**: *Bildungsplan*   105 **rally**: come together in order to help or support sb./sth.   109 **subterfuge** (fml): *List, Vorwand*   **denial**: refusal to accept that sth. unpleasant is true

chose to pretend Pakistan was doing no such thing. When Soviet forces pulled out of Afghanistan in 1989, Pakistan was left with more than 3 million Afghan refugees and a generation brought up with the culture of jihad. Then, in 1990, Pakistan's nuclear program
115 was finally recognized, and the U.S., which had already cut aid, imposed sanctions on Islamabad. "You used us, and then you dumped us," says Qadir, the retired general, echoing national sentiment. "And Pakistanis are convinced you are going to do it again."
120   [...] After 9/11, sanctions were lifted and aid restarted, with the Pakistani military again serving as the main conduit. In exchange, Islamabad would enable the free flow of supplies to NATO troops in Afghanistan, allow covert U.S. operations against terrorist groups sheltered in Pakistan and mop up any groups that threatened U.S.
125 interests. Musharraf's replacement by a civilian government in 2008 didn't change the terms of the deal, but it coincided with growing concern in the U.S. that the Pakistanis were not keeping up their end of the bargain. While Pakistan was indeed doing battle against some terrorist groups, it also seemed to allow others to thrive: the
130 Haqqani network, a group affiliated with al-Qaeda and which has attacked U.S. and NATO positions in Afghanistan, has safe haven in Pakistani territory. In the past two years, a succession of top U.S. officials have openly suggested that some of the most wanted terrorists were being sheltered by elements of the Pakistani
135 establishment.

Since the killing of bin Laden, the Obama Administration has been careful not to finger Pakistan's government or military leadership. But the bargain struck in 2001 seems to have broken down. "Clearly, from an operational perspective, the fact that the

---

117 **dump sb.** (infml): leave sb. without help or support   121 **conduit** ['kɑːnduət] (fml): thing that is used to pass money, information, etc. to other people
123 **covert** (fml): secret or hidden   124 **mop sb. up**: capturing or kill sb. (esp. the last few people who continue to oppose you)   129 **thrive**: do well, become stronger
131 **safe haven**: a place where people are safe to live and operate   132 **succession**: a series of people   137 **finger sb.**: accuse sb. of doing something wrong

U.S. executed this raid unilaterally suggests that there's not a lot of   140
faith in that relationship anymore," says Stephen Tankel, a visiting
fellow at the Carnegie Endowment for International Peace's South
Asia program. "So this seems to me an opportunity to try to engage
with a longer-term view toward promoting civilian governance in
Pakistan."   145

Many Pakistanis would like that as well but know from history
not to hold their breath. "This is a golden opportunity for the civilian
leadership to assert themselves," says Talat Masood, a retired
lieutenant general who has long campaigned to get the military out
of government. But, he adds, "knowing their capabilities, in all   150
likelihood they will not. And that is the tragedy of Pakistan."

Why is Pakistan's civilian leadership so weak? The military is at
least partly to blame. For the past two decades it has engaged in a
campaign of divide and conquer, setting political parties at odds
with one another. It has bought media complicity – either through   155
intimidation or by threatening to cut lucrative advertising from
military-owned enterprises. When politicians persist in criticizing
the military, they are quickly silenced. […]

All of which poses an obvious question: How could an
organization that so closely monitors all aspects of Pakistani life not   160
have known that bin Laden was hiding in Abbottabad? One
explanation: it wasn't looking. "The fight against al-Qaeda was part
of the larger effort to play a role in the war on terror, but you didn't
have a dedicated al-Qaeda unit in the ISI monitoring activities in
Pakistan," explains military analyst Rifaat Hussain. "It was a classic   165
case of not paying attention to something under your nose."
Pakistanis, in truth, are less concerned that bin Laden was in their
midst than about the fact that the U.S. was able to find him there
and enter Pakistani territory without the military's knowledge. "This
leads one to a more serious question: Are our nuclear assets safe?"   170

---

140 **raid**: attack   **unilateral**: *einseitig*   149 **campaign** (v): take part in or lead a
campaign to achieve sth.   150–151 **in all likelihood**: probably   154 **set sb. at
odds with sb.**: make sb. disagree strongly with sb.   164 **ISI = Inter Services
Intelligence**: the Pakistani secret service   170 **asset**: a person or thing that is
valuable or useful

asked Pakistan's former ambassador to Afghanistan Ayaz Wazir in an opinion piece in the *News*, an English daily. […]

175 Yet if the raid in Abbottabad has taken some of the shine off the military brass, the generals can be relied upon to stoke anti-American sentiment as a diversion. […] From outrage over drone attacks to hysteria over the CIA contractor who killed a pair of Pakistanis in what appeared to be a legitimate case of self-defense, anti-U.S. rage is the military's dependable standby. "Pakistan doesn't have positive leverage over us," says Christine Fair, a Pakistan expert at Georgetown
180 University. "So [the military] creates bilateral fiascoes through their media wing and uses that to temper what Pakistan will or will not do."

One thing the military won't do is take on militants in North Waziristan, which serves as a haven for the Haqqani network. […]
185 If the military were to dedicate its army to combatting militants on its western border, it would risk leaving its eastern flank vulnerable to attack from India.

Given Pakistan's fear of India, that is a lot to ask. That fear may have been fanned by a military establishment attempting to justify
190 its outsize expenditures, but India has done little to assuage the paranoia. Indeed it contributes, massing troops on the border and, according to Western diplomats in Islamabad, sending agents into Baluchistan province, where a long-simmering ethnic separatist movement invites memories of Bangladesh. And it is India – not
195 Pakistan – that has a deal with the U.S. for the peaceful exploitation of civilian nuclear power. "From the Pakistani point of view, we are the ones playing a double game," says Pakistan expert Fair. "We

---

173 **take the shine off sb./sth.** (infml): make sb./sth. seem much less good than they/it did at first   174 **brass** (infml): the people who are in the most important positions in an organization, etc.   **stoke sth.**: *etwas schüren*   176 **CIA contractor**: sb. who works for the CIA but is not an official CIA member   178 **dependable**: reliable   **standby**: frequent choice   178–179 **positive leverage**: the ability to influence what people do   181 **temper sth. with sth.** (fml): make sth. less severe by adding sth. that has the opposite effect   190 **outsize expenditures**: *unverhältnismäßig hohe Ausgaben*   **assuage sth.** [ə'sweɪdʒ] (fml): make sth. (esp. an unpleasant feeling) less severe   193 **simmer**: *langsam köcheln*

their security concerns, saying they are not relevant. Then we ask them to move their entire military in order to wage a deeply unpopular war, and meanwhile we give India a nuclear deal. No 200 wonder they don't trust us."

Still, the awkward truth remains: The U.S. needs Pakistan. U.S. officials believe that bin Laden's death offers an opportunity to peel the Taliban away from al-Qaeda. And when that happens, Pakistan will be perfectly poised to offer its assistance. Though routinely 205 denied by Pakistani officials, it is hardly a secret that Taliban leader Mullah Mohammed Omar has been using Pakistan as a base of operations ever since he fled the U.S. invasion in 2001.

With the target date for turning over responsibility for Afghan security to the Afghan army in 2015 approaching, there is near 210 universal agreement that the Taliban will have to be involved in some sort of political reconciliation. "The Americans need the Pakistanis to negotiate in Afghanistan," says a senior Western diplomat in Islamabad. In Pakistani eyes, that justifies the policy of maintaining relations with the Taliban, says Senator Azim. "We are 215 the only ones who are accused of keeping close ties, so Pakistan is the only country that [the West] can rely on. [...] A decision has to be made. Can you use Pakistan, with all its warts? My submission is that you don't have anyone else, so you might as well use us. Not by twisting our arm or accusing us. You know, do it nicely by sitting 220 down with us and listening to our point of view. Our objective is to have a friendly government in Afghanistan. Americans want a safe, honorable exit. Let us help you."

Gilani, too, insists that the relationship can be put back on track. For example, "a drones strategy can be worked out," he says. "If 225 drone strikes are effective, then we should evolve a common strategy to win over public opinion. Our position is that the technology should be transferred to us." And, he adds, he is prepared to countenance a strategy in which the CIA would continue to use drone strikes "where they are used under our supervision" – a 230

203–204 **peel sth. away from sth**.: remove sth. from on top of sth. else
212 **reconciliation**: *Versöhnung*   218 **wart**: *Warze*   **submission**: *Eingabe,*
Vorschlag   229 **countenance sth.** (fml): tolerate sth.

departure from Pakistan's publicly stated policy of condemning drone strikes as intolerable violations of sovereignty.

What Gilani really wants is some love. Washington, he told *Time*, needs to provide his people with a visible demonstration of support
235 if it hopes to rebuild trust. The U.S., the Prime Minister says, "should do something for the public which will persuade them that it is supportive of Pakistan." As an example, he cites – of course – the U.S.-India civil nuclear agreement of 2008. "It's our public that's dying, but the deal is happening there," he says in a wounded tone.
240 "You claim there's a strategic partnership? That we're best friends?"

Then, casting his eyes up at his chandeliered ceiling, Pakistan's Prime Minister reaches for a verse. "When we passed each other, she didn't deign to even say hello," he intones, quoting the Urdu poet Mirza Ghalib. "How, then, can I believe that our parting caused her
245 any tears?"

From: Aryn Baker, Time Magazine, *12 May 2011*

---

241 **chandeliered**: *mit Kronleuchtern versehen*   243 **deign** (fml): lower yourself to do sth.

7
Timeline of events relating to Pakistan

711		The Muslim invasion of the Indian subcontinent begins. Most of the area of Pakistan becomes Muslim, while the area of India remains largely Hindu.
1799		Northern Pakistan becomes part of the Sikh Empire, as the Sikhs take power away from the Muslim rulers.
1843		Britain starts to take control over much of the area of Pakistan.
1947	14/15 August	Pakistan and India are divided into two independent countries. Millions of refugees move from one country to the other. Hundreds of thousands die in the violence that accompanies Partition. During the Cold War, India is an ally of the Soviet Union, while Pakistan is an ally of the USA.
1947	October	Pakistan sends in troops to take Kashmir from India. The prince of Kashmir declares for India, but the majority of the state is Muslim.
1949	January	A ceasefire is agreed in Kashmir, leaving the state divided between the two countries. Kashmir remains a point of contention between the two countries, as it is claimed by both.
1965	Aug/Sept	Indo-Pakistani War. Pakistan infiltrates Kashmir. India invades Pakistan. Neither side makes significant gains and a ceasefire is arranged.
1971	March–Dec	Bangladesh Liberation War. Bangladesh (formerly part of Pakistan and called East Pakistan) fights for independence from West Pakistan. India sides with Bangladesh and defeats the Pakistani Army. Bangladesh becomes an independent country.
1979	December	The Soviet Union invades Afghanistan.

1989	February	The Soviet Union is forced to leave Afghanistan.
1996	September	The Taliban, supported by Pakistan, gains control of most of Afghanistan.
1999	May-July	Indo-Pakistani War. Pakistan infiltrates Kashmir. India retaliates and forces Pakistani forces to withdraw.
2001	11 September	Terrorists from Al-Qaeda fly planes into the Twin Towers in New York and the Pentagon in Washington, killing 3000 people.
2001	October	US and UK forces aid Afghan allies to topple the Taliban in Afghanistan, as the Taliban hosts Al-Qaeda. A protracted war continues up to the present.
2001	13 December	Gunmen attack the Indian Parliament, killing 12 people. India blames militants backed by Pakistan.
2001	20 December	India mobilizes its troops along the Pakistani border. Pakistan follows suit. Tension continues for the following months.
2002	14 May	Gunmen kill 34 civilians on an army base in Indian Kashmir.
2002	October	Troops on both sides de-mobilized marking an end to the tension.
2003	19 March	The USA invades Iraq, removing the regime of Saddam Hussein.
2008	26 November	Gunmen attack various sites in Mumbai, killing 164 people.
2011	2 May	Osama bin Laden is killed in a house in Abbottabad, Pakistan, by US forces.

8
When the Towers Fell

The following poem is by the American poet Galway Kinnell.

From our high window we saw them
in their bands and blocks of light
brightening against a fading sunset,
saw them in the dark hours glittering
as if spirits inside them sat up   5
calculating profit and loss all night, saw
their tops steeped in the first yellow
of sunrise, grew so used to them
often we didn't see them, and now,
not seeing them, we see them.   10

The banker is talking to London.
Humberto is delivering breakfast sandwiches.
The trader is working the phone.
The mail sorter starts sorting the mail.
The secretary arrives, the chef,   15
The gofer, the CEO … *povres et riches*
Sages et folz, prestres et laiz
Nobles, villains, larges et chiches
Petiz et grans et beaulx et laiz …

---

16 **gofer** [ˈɡoʊfər]: a person whose job is to do small tasks in a company
16–19 **povres … laiz**: lines from "The Testament" by the French poet Francois Villon
(1431–1463), meaning "poor and rich, clever and foolish, priests and laypeople,
nobles, serfs, generous and mean, small and tall and beautiful and ugly", for all of
whom death eventually comes

20 The plane screamed low, down lower Fifth Avenue,
    lifted at the Arch, someone said, shaking the dog walkers
    in Washington Square, drove for the north tower,
    struck with a heavy thud, released a huge bright gush
    of blackened orange fire, and vanished, leaving behind
25 a hole the size and shape a cartoon plane might make
    passing through and flying away, on the far side,
    back into the realm of the imaginary.

    Some with torn clothing, some bloodied
    some limping at top speed like children
30 in a three-legged race, some half dragged,
    some intact in neat suits and dresses,
    many dusted to a ghostly whiteness,
    with eyes rubbed red as the eyes of a zahorí,
    who can see the dead under the ground,
35 they swarm, in silence, up the avenues.

    Some died while calling home to say they were O.K.
    Some called the telephone operators and were told to stay put.
    Some died after over an hour spent learning they would die.
    Some died so abruptly they may have seen death from inside it.
40 Some burned, their faces caught fire.
    Some were asphyxiated.
    Some broke windows and leaned into the sunny day.
    Some were pushed out from behind by others in flames.
    Some let themselves fall, begging gravity to speed them to the
45   ground.
    Some leapt hand in hand that their fall down the sky might happen
        more lightly.

---

21 **the Arch**: arch in Washington Square Park   29 **limp**: walk slowly or with
difficulty because your leg is injured   30 **three-legged race**: a race in which people
run in pairs, the right leg of one runner being tied to the left leg of the other
33 **zahorí** (Spanish): a person who is able to see future events or to communicate
with the dead   41 **be asphyxiated** [æsˈfɪksieɪtɪd]: die due to lack of air

At the high window where I've often stood
to think, or elude a nightmare, I meet
the single, unblinking electric glare   50
lighting the all-night lifting
and sifting for bodies, pieces of bodies, a thumb, a tooth, anything
    that is not nothing.

She stands on a corner holding his picture.
He is smiling. In the heavy smoke   55
few pass. Sorry sorry sorry.
She startles.
Suppose, across the street, that headlong stride …
or there, that man with hair so black it's purple …
And yet, suppose some evening I forgot   60
The fare and transfer, yet got by that way
Without recall, – lost yet poised in traffic.
Then I might find your eyes …
Sorry sorry good luck thank you.
On this side it is "amnesia," or forgetting the way home;   65
on the other, "invisibleness," or never entirely returning.
Hard to see past the metallic mist,
or through the canopy of supposed reality
cast over our world, bourn that no creature ever born
can pry its way back through, and no love can tear.   70

All day the towers burn and fall, burn and fall.
in a shot from New Jersey they seem like smokestacks spewing
    earth's oily remnants.

---

49 **elude sb. /sth.**: manage to avoid sb./sth, esp. in a clever way   52 **sift for sth.**:
examine sth. very carefully in order to find sth. small   58 **headlong**: quickly and
without looking where you are going   60–63 **"And yet … your eyes"**: lines from
"The Marriage of Faustus and Helen" by the American poet Hart Crane (1899–
1932)   61 **fare**: the money that you pay to travel by bus, plane, taxi, etc.
62 **poised** (adj): having a calm and confident manner and in control of your feelings
and behavior   68 **canopy**: thing that covers other things   69 **cast sth.**: throw
sth.   **bourn** (old use): border, boundary   70 **pry**: manage to force yourself through

Schwarze Milch der Frühe wir trinken sie abends
75 *wir trinken sie mittags und morgens wir trinken sie nachts*
wir trinken und trinken

They come before us now not as a likeness,
but as a corollary, a small instance in the immense
lineage of the twentieth century's history of violent death –
80 black men in the South castrated and strung up from trees,
soldiers advancing through mud at ninety thousand dead per mile,
train upon train of boxcars heading eastward shoved full to the
    corners with Jews and Roma to be enslaved or gassed,
state murder of twenty, thirty, forty million of its own,
85 state starvation of a hundred million farmers,
atomic blasts erasing cities off the earth, firebombings the same,
death marches, assassinations, disappearances,
entire countries become rubble, minefields, mass graves.
Wir schaufeln ein Grab in den Lüften da liegt man nicht eng

90 Burst jet fuel, incinerated aluminum, steel fume, crushed marble,
exploded granite, pulverized drywall, mashed concrete, berserked
plastic, crazed chemicals, scoria, rotting flesh, vapor
of the vaporized – draped over
our island up to streets regimented
95 into numbers and letters, breathed across
the great bridges to Brooklyn and the waiting sea –
astringent, miasmic, empyreumatic, sticky,
air too foul to take in, but we take it in,

74–76 **"schwarze … trinken"**: lines from "Todesfuge" by the Romanian poet Paul
Celan (1920–1970)   78 **corollary** (fml): a situation that is the natural and direct
result of another one   79 **lineage**: (here) a series of related and successive events
82 **boxcar**: a closed carriage on a train used for carrying goods   89 **"wir … eng"**:
lines from "Todesfuge" (cf. above)   90 **incinerate sth.**: burn sth. completely
91 **drywall**: *Gipskartonplatten*   **berserked**: (here) distorted so that sth. looks crazy
92 **scoria**: the leftover from the melting of metal   93 **vaporize sb./sth.**: turn sb./
sth. into gas   97 **astringent**: slightly bitter but fresh   **miasmic**: poisonous
empyreumatic [ˌempəˈruːmætək]: having the odor of burnt organic matter

too gruesome for seekers of lost beloveds
to breathe, but they breathe it and you breathe it.   100

The man doesn't look up.
The photograph hangs from his neck.
He stares at the sidewalk of flagstones
laid down in Whitman's century, curbside edges rounded
by the rasps of wheels of iron and steel: 105
the human brain envying the stones:
Nie staja sie, sa.
Nic nod to, nyslalem,
zbrzydziwszy sobie
wszystko co staje sie   110

And I thought again of those on high floors
Who knew they would burn alive, and then, burned alive.
As if there were mechanisms of death
so mutilating to existence that no one
gets over them, ever, not even the dead.   115

I sat down by the waters of the Hudson
and saw in steel letters welded to the railing posts
Whitman's words written when America
was plunging into war with itself: *City of the world! …*
Proud and passionate city – mettlesome, mad, extravagant city!   120
But when the war was over and Lincoln dead
and the dead buried, Whitman remembered:

99 **gruesome**: horrible, dreadful   103 **flagstone**: a large flat square piece of stone
that is used for floors, paths, etc   104 **Walt Whitman** (1819–1892): one of the
most influential American poets   107–110 **"nie … sie"**: lines from "Songs of a
Wanderer" by the Polish poet Aleksander Wat (1900–1967), meaning "They do
not become, they are. Nothing but that, I thought, finally loathing within myself
everything that becomes."   114 **mutilate sth.**: damage sth. very badly
117 **weld sth.**: *etwas schmeißen*   120 **mettlesome**: *feurig*

I saw battle-corpses, myriads of them,
And the white skeletons of young me, I saw them,
125 *I saw the debris and debris of all the dead soldiers of the war,*
But I saw they were not as was thought.
They themselves were fully at rest – they suffer'd not,
The living remain'd and suffer'd, the mother suffer'd,
And the wife and the child and the musing comrade suffer'd.

130 In our minds the glassy blocks succumb over and over
slamming down floor by floor into themselves,
blowing up as if in reverse, exploding

downward and rolling outward,
the way, in the days of the gods, a god
135 might rage through the streets, overtaking the fleeing.

As each tower goes down, it concentrates
into itself, transforms itself
infinitely slowly into a black hole

infinitesimally small: mass
140 without space, where each light,
each life, put out, lies down within us.

From: Galway Kinnell, Strong Is Your Hold. *Tarset: Bloodaxe Books, 2007.*

123 **myriad** (fml): an extremely large number   125 **debris** [dəˈbriː]: pieces of
wood, metal, brick, etc. that are left after sth. has been destroyed   130 **succumb**:
give in, collapse   132 **in reverse**: backwards, the wrong way round
139 **infinitesimal**: extremely small

9
Man on the Path

Early on the evening after the twin towers fell, I took the PATH to
Manhattan from Jersey City where I live. It was my first trip to the
city since the attacks. I had been moved by the quiet grief and surge
of patriotism on display on our side of the Hudson but I was not
prepared for what I saw as I came out of the 14th Street station and   5
walked down Sixth Avenue towards Houston Street.

Smoke still lingered in the air. Most stores were closed. A few
people casually walked in the middle of the street. The once-bustling
street, now closed to traffic below 14th, had turned into a long
stretch of make-shift shrines at bus stops, pay-phone booths covered   10
with "Missing" fliers, couples holding hands, and small groups
taking part in candlelight vigils. But what I was most moved by was
the display of flags. They were everywhere. Giant flags on storefront
windows, bandana flags on sidewalk vendor's foreheads, little flags
sticking out of backpacks, and piles and piles of stars and stripes on 15
the vendors' tables. As an Afghan, I'd never carried the black, red,
and green flag of my own country. Suddenly, though, I wanted to
feel what it was like to proudly hold a flag, wave it at passing
ambulances, police cars and fire trucks. It would be a good way to
show my solidarity with Americans. It was my way of saying, we're   20
in this together. I'm with you. I share your pain. So I bought a
passport-sized flag for $2, and sheepishly held it up as I walked to
the East Village to meet a friend, all the while self-conscious of the

1 **PATH = Port Authority Trans-Hudson**: a subway service that connects
Manhattan with stations in New Jersey   3 **surge**: a sudden increase in sth.
8 **bustling**: full of people moving about in a busy way   10 **shrine**: a place that
people visit because it is connected with sb./sth. important to them   12 **vigil**:
Nachtwache   14 **bandana**: a piece of brightly coloured cloth worn around the neck
or head   16 **vendor**: a person who sells things, usu. outside on the street
22 **sheepish**: feeling embarrassed

incongruous spectacle of a Non-Resident Alien carrying an American
25 flag. What am I doing, holding an American flag? I don't even have a
Green Card.

But as I passed some angry-looking vendors who seemed to be
studying the faces of every passer-by, I realized that the flag could
serve a larger purpose than an awkward show of patriotism. It would
30 give me a sense of security at a time when my co-religionists were
drawing the violent ire of bigots around the country. It would help
me blend in with the native crowd. I've always been a proud Afghan,
but on this evening walking down Avenue of the Americas in my
GAP khakis and Brook Brothers buttoned-down shirt purchased at
35 the World Trade Center, I feared that someone might ask me where I
was from, mistake me for an Arab.

"It's good protection," my friend said later, when she saw my flag.
"I guess," I said, "but I didn't buy it for that reason."

When I got to the PATH station the following evening, the rush-
40 hour crowd had thinned out. I was still carrying my flag. It was
unusually bright inside. The two benches had been removed from
the middle of the platform, and the "World Trade Center" sign had
been switched off. As I walked to the far end of the platform, a 33rd
Street train pulled in. I stepped into the car, sat down, and surveyed
45 the handful of people inside. No one I should be on guard for,
I concluded.

Everyone looked tired. A young, scraggly couple sat at the other
end of the car in silence. Across from them, an old man under a
"Drug-Free New Jersey" poster, next to them two young Asian
50 women and a white man, and closest to the central door, a young
man by himself, quietly reading a little book.

On any other day, I'd not have looked at the man twice, but
something about him piqued my interest. He wore an outsize black

---

24 **incongruous**: strange, and not suitable in a particular situation   26 **Green
Card**: a legal document that allows somebody from another country to live and
work in the USA   31 **ire** ['aɪr] (fml): anger, wrath   **bigot**: a person who has very
strong, unreasonable opinions about race, religion or politics   47 **scraggly**: *zottelig*
53 **pique sb.'s interest**: make sb. very interested in sth.

coat and dark slacks, and sported a long, neatly trimmed beard. He
was hunched over a little, leather-bound book that he held in both   55
hands. I couldn't make out the book. But as he looked up
momentarily, I could see his deep, dark eyes behind his glasses. He
had a light complexion. I looked at him closely. He could have
passed as an Orthodox Jew but there was something un-Orthodox
about him. The missing yarmulke. He was not wearing a yarmulke   60
or an Orthodox hat. Still, I couldn't be sure. I couldn't tell if he
looked European or Arab. He could be Egyptian, I thought, or a
Ukrainian Orthodox Jew.

It was not an uncommon sight on the PATH, a bearded Muslim,
and sometimes a clean-shaved one, reading the Koran on late-night   65
rides, or an Orthodox Jew perched over his Bible. I never made
much of them. But it was two days after America had come under
attack, and Muslims were keeping a low profile. The local falafel
shop in my neighborhood had yet to reopen, the cab stand was
empty of its mostly Arab drivers, and the Arab shoe repairman near   70
my apartment had plastered an enormous American flag on his
window. It would be rude, foolish, even reckless, for a Muslim to
flaunt his faith in such an overt way on this particular evening,
I thought.

My curiosity increased as the train neared the Christopher Street   75
station in Manhattan, and the man continued his quiet reading
without looking up. I got up from my seat to steal a glance at his
book. As I walked past him, he was still hunched over his book, but
I could see the distinct Arabic letters on its cream-colored pages. The
book was bound in a zip-up black leather case. It was the Koran.   80
I was stunned. What did he think he was doing? Wasn't he afraid?
What he was doing was suicidal. The train went on to 14th Street,
my stop. As I got off, I could see the man still engrossed in his

---

54 **slacks** (AE): trousers that are not part of a suit   60 **yarmulke** ['jɑːrmʊlkə]: a
small round cap worn on top of the head by Jewish men   68 **keep a low profile**:
nicht auffällig verhalten   73 **flaunt sth.**: show you are proud of sth. to other people
in order to impress them   80 **zip-up leather case**: *mit Reißverschluss verschließbarer
Ledereinband*   82 **suicidal**: very dangerous and likely to lead to death   83 **engross
sb.**: be so interesting that you give it all your attention and time

reading, at peace with himself. He shifted in his seat slightly but
didn't look up even though, as I thought, he was aware of my
intrusive eyes.

I wanted to talk to him, ask him if he was afraid, but I knew what
his answer would be. Why should I be afraid? I'm not a terrorist.
Why should I hide my religion? I'm a Muslim and I'm not afraid of
practicing my religion. I read the Koran because I love it and because
it's every Muslim's religious duty. The Prophet said reading the Koran
cleanses the heart. God will protect you when you're in danger, and
when the time to go comes, it comes. No one can stop it.

He had kept, on the PATH train to Manhattan, what I had learned
as a Muslim but had since lost. I have not carried the flag since.

From: Masood Favrivar. In: 110 Stories. New York Writes after
September 11. *Ulrich Baer (ed.). New York: New York University Press, 2002*

176

The Author

Mohsin Hamid (born 1971) was born in Lahore, Pakistan. He spent part of his childhood in the USA, while his father, a university professor, was studying for a PhD at Stanford University in California. The family then moved back to Lahore, where he attended the Lahore American School.

At the age of 18, Hamid returned to the USA to study at Princeton University, where he studied international relations. He also enrolled in courses in creative writing under such writers as Joyce Carol Oates and Toni Morrison. Hamid attended Harvard Law School, graduating in 1997. He then worked for several years as a management consultant at McKinsey & Company in New York City. In 2001 he moved to London, and then to Lahore in 2009 with his wife and daughter.

His first novel, *Moth Smoke* (2000), is the story of a marijuana-smoking ex-banker in post-nuclear-test Lahore who falls in love with his best friend's wife. His second novel, *The Reluctant Fundamentalist* (2007) became an international bestseller, and was shortlisted for the Man Booker Prize. It has been translated into over 25 languages. Hamid has also written on politics, art, literature, travel, and other topics in various newspapers and magazines around the world.